ONCE UPON A

BAGEL

WHAT WILL YOU EAT ON YOUR BAGEL TODAY?

ONCE UPON A BAGEL

WHAT WILL YOU EAT ON YOUR BAGEL TODAY?

BY JAY HARLOW

ILLUSTRATIONS BY EVE ALDRIDGE

HARLOW & RATNER

EMERYVILLE, CALIFORNIA

FOR REBECCA
AND HER GRANDMA AND GRANDPA

Interior and Cover Design: McClain Design
Typography: SharmanDesign

Library of Congress Cataloging-in-Publication Data

Harlow, Jay. 1953-
    Once upon a bagel : what will you eat on your bagel today? / by
Jay Harlow ; illustrations by Eve Aldridge.
         p.   cm.
    Includes index.
    ISBN 1-883791-01-4 : $10.95
    1. Cookery (Bagels)   2. Bagels.   I. Title
TX770.B35H37 1994   94-34557
641.8'15--dc20   .   CIP

Printed in Singapore

10 9 8 7 6 5 4 3 2

Harlow & Ratner
5749 Landregan Street
Emeryville, CA 94608

ACKNOWLEDGMENTS

Thanks to the following people who helped me in putting together this book:

Noah Alper of Noah's Bagels, Emeryville, CA, and Gail Hutton and William Powell of Brothers' Bagels, Berkeley, CA, for their time in explaining the bagel baking process to me. Joan Nathan, for historical help.

For sharing recipe ideas, John Shields, chef of Saul's Delicatessen and Restaurant, Berkeley, CA; also my mother, Phoebe Harlow, and mother-in-law, Evelyn Ratner. Susan Mattmann and Matt Morse, for lending me their kitchen at a crucial stage in the recipe testing.

Dan McClain, for a great design, Eve Aldridge, for her light-hearted illustrations, and Susan Sharman, for her fine typography.

Joan Watsabaugh, whose enthusiasm from the very start energized me to write yet another cookbook.

Elaine Ratner, my editor, wife, and partner. She suggested the book in the first place, and she kept it on the right track, curbing my natural tendency to turn a small book of recipes into a lengthy academic dissertation. She was also amazingly open-minded about my sometimes crazy ideas for how to serve bagels.

CONTENTS

RECIPES

ONCE UPON A BAGEL

Some people get misty-eyed over memories of a great joke they once told, a magnificent sunset they watched from a white-sand beach, a fish that fought for hours before surrendering. My most stirring memories tend to be about food. Once I made a souffle that rose a full four inches above the baking dish and melted in the mouth like a cloud. Once I cooked a salmon so perfectly that everyone at the table closed their eyes and sighed after the first bite, and declared it the best they had ever eaten. Once I topped a bagel...

I have put all sorts of toppings on bagels. Some were *wonderful*. Some needed work. Some I am sure would have horrified the Eastern European Jews who brought this exquisite form of bread to our shores, never dreaming that nouveau bagel fanatics like me would pile them high with such nontraditional toppings as chicken salad and watercress. Let me make one thing clear. I am fond of cream cheese. I love lox (smoked salmon to the uninitiated). I have eaten hundreds of bagels with cream cheese and lox and relished every bite. But have you ever tried a bagel with cream cheese and chutney? Or mixed little tiny bits of jalapeño chile into your cream cheese before spreading it on? Have you ever topped a bagel with baba ganoush?

Bagels are so delicious, so adaptable, so inspiring — it would be a shame to always top them with cream cheese and lox. So, with heartfelt thanks and sincere apologies to the bagel inventors of Europe, and their descendants who carried their precious recipes to New York City and from there to every part of America, I continue my often unconventional, occasionally non-kosher, but always respectful explorations of the dozens and dozens of mouthwatering things that taste great on a bagel.

WHAT IT MEANS
TO BE A BAGEL LOVER

It has been said you are what you eat. People who eat bagels should take that as a compliment. Bagels are good looking, substantial, and spirited. When you hold a bagel in your hand, you know you're holding something solid. Something that's going to deliver. You know you've chosen well, and you are about to be rewarded.

In my experience, people who eat bagels are adventuresome, good humored, and fun. They demand more from life, and from every meal. They love to travel and to eat the great foods of the world. Like bagels. And all the wonderful things you can put on bagels.

Which brings me to the subject we are here to explore: what should you eat on your bagel?

THE BAGEL IS AN AMERICAN CITIZEN

The bagel came to the United States from Eastern Europe, as did many American immigrants. Slowly it gained in popularity, moving from the cities of the Northeast to the West Coast, then spreading from both coasts into the middle of the country. Today bagels are sold in every part of America, in supermarkets as well as bakeries and delicatessens. Bagels have become as American as apple pie and pizza.

Like pizza, bagels in America have become an arena of self-expression. Old World conservatism, which favored a few simple bagel variations and topped them with cream cheese and lox and maybe a slice of onion, has given way to good old American ingenuity and individualism. Now bagels come in flavors: not just rye, poppy seed, onion, and garlic, but cinnamon-raisin, blueberry, chocolate chip. I used to draw the line at blueberry bagels, but now I buy them because they're my daughter's favorite. How can I criticize her love for blueberry bagels when I'm eating avocado, jicama, and grapefruit on my poppy seed bagel?

Which brings us to the question you're waiting for me to answer: what should you eat on your bagel?

UNITED BY BAGELS

Bagel lovers have a lot in common, regardless of ethnic or regional background. At my local bagel store, the line that snakes down the sidewalk every Sunday morning is as multi-ethnic as the city we live in. We all come together on Sunday morning in a convincing demonstration of our common bonds. We all want to start the day with bagels. What we put on our bagels in the privacy of our homes may differ greatly. But, whether you top your bagel with cream cheese or mozzarella, with lox or turkey, with onions or chiles, if you are a bagel lover you are a member of a loyal and tightly knit group. You will be back next Sunday morning, and so will I.

If you don't have a bagel store in your neighborhood, that's okay. You have a supermarket. You have a grocery store. You are one of us too. Whether you buy your bagels on Sunday or Wednesday or every day, bagel lovers are bagel lovers. We are a group, large and growing larger. We are united by our hunger for real satisfaction and our good taste.

Which makes me think I had better turn to the subject at hand: what should you eat on your bagel?

AN IMPORTANT NOTE TO PARENTS OF SMALL CHILDREN

Nobody else cares about this, but if your child is teething, or going to be teething soon, you should know that stale bagels are the best teething rings ever made. (Our friend Gerry Dunn taught us that.) Get a plain bagel and hide it so it has time to get stale — a couple of days is enough. Then, when the bawling begins (teething really hurts), pull out the bagel and thrust it into his (or her) little hand. Watch him gnaw. Listen to the sweet silence.

Now, what are you going to eat on your bagel? Here come the recipes.

BAGEL AND CREAM CHEESE

A smear of cream cheese is the most basic topping for a bagel. Make it as thick or thin as your taste and diet dictate. See page 113 for information about varieties of cream cheese. For a lower-fat alternative, see the recipe for Fromage Blanc on page 12.

———————

1 bagel, split
1 to 2 tablespoons cream cheese

Toast the bagel if you like, or warm it in the oven. (You don't have to do either if the bagel is good and fresh.) Spread with cream cheese. Serve open face.

Makes 1 bagel

Good with any kind of bagel.

———————

For many bagel lovers, a bagel just isn't complete without smoked salmon, also known as lox. How much lox to use can be more a matter of price than taste. How you put it on is a matter of personal style. Some people lay their lox ceremoniously on top of the cream cheese, careful to preserve the integrity of each slice. Others spread it aggressively into the cheese, breaking it up to make sure there is some in every bite. It's up to you. Home-Cured Salmon (page 30) and Gravlax (page 31) can be used interchangeably with lox.

---

1 bagel, split
1 to 2 tablespoons cream cheese
Thinly sliced smoked salmon (see page 114)
Optional garnishes:
Thinly sliced raw onion or Pickled Onion Rings (page 59)
Sliced tomato
A few capers or a squeeze of lemon

Toast or warm the bagel, if you like. Spread it with cream cheese and top with salmon. Add your choice of garnish.

Makes 1 bagel

Good with any kind of bagel.

FROMAGE BLANC

This really low-fat substitute for cream was introduced to many American cooks by French chef Paul Bocuse in his revolutionary 1976 book *Cuisine Minceur*. It can also mimic cream cheese. When made with low-fat ricotta, it has less than one-fifth the fat of regular cream cheese; made with whole-milk ricotta, it has about a third as much fat. Of course, the more fat in the ricotta, the richer and creamier the taste.

---

1 cup ricotta (whole milk or part skim)
1 tablespoon plain yogurt

Combine the ricotta and yogurt in a food processor or blender and blend, stopping frequently to scrape down the sides, until the texture is as smooth as possible. This may take several minutes; the smoother the texture the better. Pack the *fromage blanc* into a storage container (the rinsed-out ricotta container will work fine), cover, and refrigerate up to a week.

Makes 1 cup

YOGURT CHEESE

This is absolutely the leanest alternative to cream cheese, and it takes just a few minutes to make. I had heard about it for a long time and finally tried it when I saw it in an article by Anne Sterling in *Fine Cooking* magazine. It's easy and tasty, and it's going to be a staple in my refrigerator. Use it as is, or mixed with cream cheese to reduce the fat, or in place of all or part of the cream cheese in mixed spreads.

---

1 pint plain low-fat or nonfat yogurt (without gelatin)
¼ teaspoon kosher salt

Line a large funnel or clean coffee filter cone with a large (6-cup) paper coffee filter. Set it over a tall jar. Combine the yogurt and salt and place the mixture in the filter. Cover the whole contraption with plastic wrap and put it in the refrigerator overnight. In 8 to 24 hours the whey will have drained away, leaving cheese with a consistency somewhere between sour cream and cream cheese. Remove the cheese from the filter and wrap it tightly. Use it within 3 or 4 days.

Makes 1 scant cup

STRAWBERRY CREAM CHEESE

Calorie counters rejoice! Mixing low-fat yogurt cheese with the cream cheese in this recipe actually makes it taste better. Vary the proportion of the two cheeses to suit your taste. Remember that more yogurt may require more sugar to balance the flavors.

¼ cup cream cheese
⅓ cup Yogurt Cheese (page 13)
3 or 4 large strawberries
Sugar to taste

Combine the cheeses in a bowl and beat until smooth and well blended. Dice enough strawberries to make ½ cup, then chop them fine and stir them into the cheese. Add a pinch of sugar, or more to taste. Let stand an hour or two for the best flavor, but use within a day or two.

Makes 1 cup

Best on plain, whole wheat, multigrain, sesame, or poppy bagels.

PRUNE CREAM CHEESE

Prunes always seem to get a chuckle. But this enormous raisin (made from a plum rather than a grape) is sweet and moist, and it tastes great mixed with cream cheese. Just don't eat too much. Or too many raisins, or too much of any dried fruit for that matter.

---

6 good-sized pitted prunes
4 ounces cream cheese

If the prunes are especially dry, soak them in water for 15 minutes, then drain well and pat them dry. Beat the cream cheese by hand or in a mixer until light. Chop the prunes as fine as possible and fold them into the cheese.

Makes ½ cup

Good on most bagels, perhaps not garlic or onion.

GINGER-PECAN CREAM CHEESE

Mixing nuts and cream cheese can be tricky. I don't know why, but cream cheese brings out a bitterness in the skins of walnuts. Pecans have a gentler, less tannic flavor that works better. Crystallized ginger varies a lot in flavor, so adjust the amount to taste.

---

2 ounces cream cheese
2 tablespoons pecans, chopped
2 teaspoons finely chopped crystallized ginger

Beat the cream cheese by hand or in a mixer until light. Work in the chopped pecans and ginger with a spatula. Use within a day or two, before the nuts lose their crunch.

Makes ⅓ cup, enough for 2 to 3 bagels

APRICOT-ALMOND CREAM CHEESE

Apricots and almonds have a natural flavor affinity. Plump, moist Turkish dried apricots are best for this recipe, if you can find them. Domestic dried apricots are often much drier, and may need soaking to soften them up. For a lower-fat spread, replace up to half of the cream cheese with Yogurt Cheese (page 13).

---

4 ounces cream cheese
6 dried apricots
1 to 2 tablespoons toasted slivered almonds

Beat the cream cheese by hand or in a mixer until light. Chop the apricots and almonds as fine as possible and fold them into the cheese. Use within 2 or 3 days or the almonds will lose their crunch. (They'll still taste good.)

Makes ⅔ cup

ANISE-ALMOND CREAM CHEESE

If you like to dunk Italian biscotti in your coffee or milk, as I do, you already know how wonderful the subtle combination of anise and almond can make a cookie. Discover what the same combination of flavors can do for a bagel.

---

1 tablespoon slivered almonds
1 teaspoon anise seeds
2 ounces cream cheese
½ teaspoon sugar

Toast the almonds in a dry skillet over medium-low heat until golden brown, shaking the pan frequently once they begin to show color. Remove them from the pan and let them cool. Toast the anise seeds in the same pan until fragrant. Chop the almonds fine, and the anise seeds so that each seed is at least cracked open. Stir both into the cream cheese and add the sugar.

Makes ⅓ cup, enough for 2 bagels

Best on plain or egg bagels.

BRAMBLEBERRY CREAM CHEESE

Use whatever "brambleberries" are available — blackberries, raspberries, Boysenberries, ollalieberries, Marionberries, or Loganberries. Each berry gives the spread a slightly different hue, from the gentle pink of raspberries to the screaming magenta of some blackberries. The natural sweetness will vary considerably, so taste the puree before adding any sugar. Frozen unsweetened berries will work fine; the kind frozen in syrup may be too sweet.

¼ cup fresh or thawed berries
½ teaspoon sugar, or to taste
4 ounces cream cheese, preferably whipped

Place the berries in a wire sieve over a bowl and mash them with a spoon, forcing all the juice and pulp through the sieve and leaving the seeds behind. Taste the puree for sweetness and add sugar as necessary. Add the cream cheese and stir and mash with a fork or rubber spatula until thoroughly combined.

Makes ½ cup

Good on plain, poppy, or sesame bagels, warm or toasted.

JALAPEÑO CREAM CHEESE

If your supermarket sells bagels it probably sells fresh jalapeños. Buy several. Chiles vary tremendously in heat and the only way to tell how much punch a particular chile has is to taste it. Slit one in half lengthwise, cut off a thin sliver including some of the inner ribs, and touch it to the tip of your tongue. You'll know in an instant if it's a real firecracker or a dud. If it's too mild, try another one. If it's too hot, carefully remove every trace of the ribs and seeds (where most of the heat is) and try again; it may be just right. You can substitute other small chiles, including the smaller serrano and the larger red or green Fresno. If it's more convenient, buy a jar of Mexican pickled jalapeños *(jalapeños en escabeche)*; they will keep for months in the refrigerator.

---

4 ounces cream cheese
1 fresh jalapeño chile, seeded and minced
or 1 pickled chile, drained, halved, and minced
1 tablespoon minced sweet red pepper (optional)
Pinch of sugar

Combine everything and let stand 1 hour.
Taste. Add more chile if you want.
In fall and winter it's nice to sprinkle a few
pomegranate seeds on top as a garnish.

Makes ½ cup

Variation:
Spread the bagels with plain cream cheese
and top with jalapeño jelly.

Best on plain, egg, or sesame bagels.

TAPENADE CREAM CHEESE

Tapenade, an intensely flavorful black olive spread, is one of the distinctive flavors of Provençal cooking. John Shields, chef of Saul's Delicatessen in Berkeley, California, uses typical tapenade ingredients to spike one of his popular cream cheese spreads. This is his recipe. Feel free to adjust the ratio of cream cheese to tapenade to suit your taste. (I like it on the strong side.)

---

8 Kalamata olives, pitted
3 sun-dried tomato halves
1 teaspoon capers
1 anchovy filet or 1 teaspoon anchovy paste
½ teaspoon chopped garlic
2 tablespoons fresh basil leaves
½ pound cream cheese (approximately)

Chop everything but the cream cheese together as finely as possible. Mix half of this mixture (tapenade) and half of the cream cheese in a bowl with a rubber spatula. Add in more cheese and more tapenade to get the taste balance you like. Cover and refrigerate overnight for the fullest flavor.

Makes ½ to 1 cup, enough for lots of bagels

Best on sesame, poppy, or other "plain-vanilla" bagels.

WATERCRESS AND CHEESE

Let's start a movement to liberate watercress from those prissy little tea sandwiches. This pungent, peppery green is a perfect companion to the earthy flavor of rye or pumpernickel bagels. If you've always pushed the watercress garnish aside in nice restaurants, without ever even tasting it, you're in for a happy surprise.

---

1 bunch watercress
⅔ cup cream cheese or Fromage Blanc (page 12)
Salt, to taste
2 bagels, split

Remove and throw away the bruised lower leaves and heavy stems from 4 or 5 sprigs of watercress. Wash the sprigs by plunging them in a bowl of water. Lift them out, pat dry, and chop coarsely. Stir half of the chopped watercress into the cheese and add a little salt. Spread the cheese on the bagel halves and scatter the remaining watercress on top.

Makes 2 bagels

Best on rye or pumpernickel bagels.

TOASTED BAGEL WITH CHEESE

Yes, this is ridiculously simple. It's also endlessly variable and always satisfying. If you have a toaster, you can have a hot lunch. But (there *is* a tough part) getting the cheese perfectly melted takes split-second timing. Be sure you have everything ready before you go near the toaster.

---

2 ounces (approximately) cheese of your choice
1 bagel, split

Use any cheese that slices easily and melts well:
cheddar types (including jack, Colby, Cheshire), Swiss types,
Danish Havarti with or without herbs or spices, Fontina or any of
its imitators, Port Salut or other French semisoft cheeses, Bel Paese,
mozzarella or provolone, Dutch Edam or Gouda.

I don't recommend cheeses that crumble, like feta, many blue
cheeses, hard grating cheeses like Parmesan, or really soft cheeses.
Also, I don't think heating does much for the flavor of Brie,
Camembert, and other white-rind cheeses.

Slice enough cheese to make as thick a layer as you like and lay it
out on a plate to begin to warm up. Toast the bagel halves, and
within seconds after they pop up, rush them onto the plate and top
them with the cheese. When it has melted to your liking, enjoy.

Makes 1 bagel

SUN-DRIED TOMATO SPREAD

Drying tomatoes in the sun transforms their flavor and texture, intensifying their sweetness *and* their tartness. (Think how grapes change in becoming raisins.) A bit of chopped dried tomato makes plain cream cheese so intensely flavorful, I think it's too much for breakfast bagels.

If you have oil-packed dried tomatoes, you can skip the steeping step. Just pull some out of the jar, drain off as much oil as possible, and chop.

---

4 dried tomato halves
4 ounces cream cheese (regular or low-fat)

Put the dried tomatoes in a small pot with about ⅛ inch of water. Bring to a boil, cover, turn off the heat, and let steep until the tomatoes are soft and swollen, about 15 minutes. Drain on a paper towel and let cool. Chop finely and blend with the cream cheese.

Makes ½ cup

Best on onion, sesame, or poppy seed bagels.

SCRAMBLED EGG AND CHEESE

Take those scrambled eggs you like so much at breakfast, put them on a bagel, add some cheese, and you've got a tasty brunch, lunch, or supper dish that you can eat with your hands. Use whatever good melting cheese you like. Some good choices: jack, cheddar, Fontina, Bel Paese, Port Salut.

---

2 eggs
¼ cup minced green onion
Large pinch of salt and pepper
1 tablespoon butter or oil
2 bagels, split and lightly toasted
4 slices cheese

Beat the eggs lightly with the onion, salt, and pepper. Melt the butter in a nonstick skillet over medium heat and add the eggs. Cook, stirring gently once the eggs begin to thicken, until they are evenly set but still moist. Set the bagel halves on a cookie sheet. Divide the eggs into quarters and gently lift one quarter onto each bagel half. Top with cheese. Slip under the broiler until the cheese is melted and beginning to brown. Serve hot or warm.

Zippy Variation:
In addition to or instead of the cheese on top, stir about 2 tablespoons of crumbled feta cheese into the eggs just before they come out of the pan.

Makes 2 bagels

CUCUMBER AND CHEESE BAGEL

If you make this with yogurt cheese, it's almost fat-free. If you don't have time to make the yogurt cheese, whip a little cream cheese and plain nonfat yogurt together; the cucumbers really need the sour tang the yogurt gives. Try to get one of those thin-skinned, individually wrapped "English" or "hothouse" cucumbers. They're a little more expensive than ordinary cucumbers, but they don't need to be seeded or peeled. If all you can get is the thicker waxed type, peel it first, and slice off an end to see how it looks inside. If the seeds are large, split the cuke lengthwise and scrape out the seeds, then cut it into crescent-shaped slices.

¼ medium cucumber, thinly sliced
Salt
1 bagel, split
2 tablespoons Yogurt Cheese (page 13)
Black pepper, hot paprika, or cayenne (optional)

Place the cucumber slices in a small bowl and sprinkle with a little salt. Toss to distribute the salt evenly. Let stand about 2 minutes, then spread the slices on a paper towel to drain. Spread the bagel halves with cheese, sprinkle with a little pepper if you like, and arrange a layer of overlapping cucumber slices on top.

Makes 1 bagel

Countless jars of homemade chutney are given as gifts every year. If you know someone who does home canning, chances are you have a jar or two on hand. Consider yourself blessed. Chutney is a great bagel topping. If you're not on a home canner's gift list, buy yourself a jar of commercially made chutney (try Major Grey's if you like mango).

**2 tablespoons cream cheese
or Fromage Blanc (page 12)
2 to 3 teaspoons chutney**

Split a bagel and spread each half with cheese. Top with chutney.

Makes 1 bagel

Best on sesame, cinnamon raisin, multigrain, or plain bagels.
Not so good on rye or onion bagels.

LOX SHMEER

"Shmeer" is Yiddish for spread. (If you don't know much about Yiddish, try reading Leo Rosten's wonderful *The Joys of Yiddish* while you "nosh" on bagels. It will put you in the right mood, and laughter is good for the digestion.) Combining cream cheese and lox into a shmeer makes them easier and less expensive to apply to your bagels. Use lox trim pieces. The more delicate (and expensive) types of lox aren't strong enough in flavor.

---

4 ounces cream cheese
1 ounce belly lox or smoked salmon trim (see page 114), chopped
1 teaspoon minced fresh dill (optional)

Beat the cheese with a spoon or rubber spatula until it's soft and light. Stir in the salmon, and dill if you like it. When all is well blended, pack the shmeer into a small container, cover it tightly, and refrigerate 1 hour before serving. It will keep up to 7 days in the refrigerator.

Makes ⅔ cup, enough for 3 to 4 bagels

Best on bagels that are not sweet.

The smoked fish that have become identified with bagels — lox, Nova salmon, and sometimes smoked sturgeon — are cold-smoked. But many more kinds of smoked fish are hot-smoked. Fully cooked in the smoking process, they have the firmer, drier texture of cooked fish. Hot-smoked whitefish, trout, tuna, bluefish, and "kippered" salmon are all delicious on bagels. They will crumble if sliced as thin as lox; flake them apart or cut fairly thick slices.

½ teaspoon prepared horseradish (optional)
2 tablespoons cream cheese
1 bagel, split
1 to 2 ounces hot-smoked fish

Mix the horseradish into the cheese, if you like. Spread it on the bagel halves and top with smoked fish. If the pieces of fish are in danger of falling off, press them into the cheese with the spreading knife.

Makes 1 bagel

HOME-CURED SALMON

It's easier than you might think to cure salmon at home. This salmon isn't smoked. Its flavor is similar to traditional lox, but less salty. And it costs about half of what you'd pay at the deli. If you want to impress your guests at Sunday brunch, buy your fish on Wednesday or Thursday. The recipe takes just a half hour to prepare, but the salmon has to cure in the refrigerator for two or three days. Please read the Gravlax recipe on page 31 for important information about what kind of fish is safest for home curing.

---

1 pound salmon filet, in one piece with skin on
¼ cup kosher salt
2 tablespoons brown sugar
½ teaspoon ground white pepper

Look over the filet for any pin bones — the long, thin bones that look like white spots on the surface. Grasp the end of each bone with clean tweezers or needle-nose pliers and pull it out with a quick tug. Rinse the filet and pat it dry.

Place the fish skin side down in a glass or stainless dish. Combine the salt, sugar, and pepper and spread them evenly all over the fish, a bit heavier on the thicker part. Cover loosely with plastic wrap and set another pan on top. Put 2 to 3 pounds of weight inside the top pan (a jar of mayonnaise, a bottle of wine) to weight the fish down. Place the whole set-up in the refrigerator, with something under one end to tilt it slightly. Leave 2 to 3 days, then rinse off the surface salt and soak the fish in fresh water for 15 minutes. Drain thoroughly, pat dry, and wrap tightly. Your cured salmon will keep for another 3 to 5 days. Serve like lox, sliced thinly on the diagonal.

Makes 1 pound, enough for plenty of bagels

GRAVLAX

This Scandinavian version of cured salmon is sweeter than lox and is flavored with fresh dill. The curing procedure is the same as in the previous recipe. Farm-raised Atlantic salmon (often labeled "Norwegian" even when it comes from Canada, Maine, or Washington) is the safest to use for curing raw fish at home. Wild salmon sometimes carry parasites which are not killed in the curing process. You can also use large red-meated rainbow trout farmed in fresh water.

---

1 pound salmon filet, in one piece with skin on
3 tablespoons kosher salt
3 tablespoons brown sugar
½ teaspoon ground white pepper
½ cup chopped fresh dill

Follow the procedure for Home-Cured Salmon (page 30), adding a thick layer of dill on top of the salt, sugar, and pepper. Do not rinse after curing. When slicing, include a little of the dill with each slice.

Makes 1 pound, enough for plenty of bagels

Canned sardines are one of the great convenience foods. You can open the can, mash them with a fork, mix in a little mayonnaise, and you've got a sardine equivalent of tuna or salmon salad. I don't do that. I prefer to present my sardines intact and carefully laid out, whether on a plate or on top of a bagel.

For the best appearance, look for sardine cans labeled "double layer." That means there are lots of small fish inside rather than four or five big ones. Sardines this size generally come from Norway rather than this side of the Atlantic.

---

2 bagels, split
2 tablespoons softened butter *or* 4 tablespoons cream cheese
2 or 3 tender lettuce leaves, shredded
1 can sardines (double layer pack)
Lemon wedges (optional)

Spread the bagel halves with butter or cream cheese. Add a thin layer of shredded lettuce and arrange the sardines on top. Squeeze on a little lemon juice if you like.

Makes 2 bagels

Best on pumpernickel or rye bagels.

PICKLED HERRING

Pickled herring comes in almost as many "flavors" as bagels. Use your favorite, whether it's plain, in wine, in sour cream, with mustard sauce — whatever. You'll find some types of pickled herring chilled in bulk in delis or in jars in supermarkets. Other types come in cans that can be stored for months at room temperature. I have even tasted a version from Germany that is canned in lobster-flavored sauce. They are all good on bagels.

---

2 to 3 ounces pickled herring
1 bagel, split
1 to 2 tablespoons cream cheese
Butter lettuce or other tender lettuce leaves

If the herring pieces are large enough, cut them crosswise into slices that look like small salmon steaks. Leave smaller chunks or filet pieces as is. Spread the bagel halves with a little cream cheese, then arrange herring pieces on top. Add some of the onions or anything else packed with the herring that looks good. Finish with a lettuce leaf on top, to help you hold everything in place without getting your fingers dirty.

Makes 1 bagel

CHOPPED HERRING

This recipe comes from my mother-in-law, who learned it from her mother...and who knows how many generations it goes back. If (like me) you don't much like green pepper, substitute red bell pepper, which is the same thing only fully ripe. Herring is traditionally chopped in a wooden bowl with a curved chopping knife. An old-fashioned meat grinder is also traditional, and does a nice job, but it tends to leak all over the floor. You will do very well with a cutting board and a chef's knife. You can also use a food processor, but your herring won't look the same. (For some reason, it comes out paler.) You might want to mash everything together with a fork at the end to get a spreadable consistency.

---

1 good-sized slice white bread
½ pint herring in wine sauce
½ medium sweet pepper, seeded
1 apple, peeled
½ medium onion, peeled
1 rib celery
1 hard-cooked egg
Pinch of sugar (optional)
1 tablespoon mild vegetable oil

Put the bread in a bowl and drain the liquid from the herring over it. Grind or chop the pepper, apples, onion, celery, and egg together finely. Chop the herring and soaked bread a little less fine and add them in. Taste for sugar; the apple, onion, and herring brine may be sweet enough, but if not add sugar to taste. Stir in a little oil. Cover and chill if not serving immediately. Spread on warm or room-temperature bagels.

Makes 2 cups, enough for 4 to 6 bagels

SHRIMP OR LOBSTER SALAD

Spicy Louisiana rémoulade sauce goes well with all kinds of crustaceans. The dressing on this salad is a somewhat toned-down version. Make your salad with tiny whole shrimp, larger shrimp cut into small cubes, or lobster tails sliced crosswise into coin-shaped pieces. Cooked crab chunks are also good. If you use frozen, already cooked shellfish, be sure to drain it well as it thaws or its juices will thin down the dressing.

---

1 tablespoon mayonnaise
1 tablespoon Yogurt Cheese (page 13) or plain yogurt
1 tablespoon chopped parsley or celery leaves
1 tablespoon minced green onion
¼ teaspoon dried tarragon, crumbled
Knife-tip of hot paprika or cayenne
⅓ pound cooked shrimp or lobster meat

Combine all the ingredients except the shellfish in a bowl and mix well. Taste for seasoning and adjust if necessary. (Bear in mind that the pepper flavor will get hotter as it stands.) Cut the shellfish into conveniently sized pieces and stir it into the dressing. Spread the salad on bagel halves.

Makes enough for 2 bagels

Best on poppy, sesame, or pumpernickel bagels.

SALMON SALAD

Living near San Francisco, I eat a lot of fresh salmon (they are caught right outside the Golden Gate). If your market sells salmon fresh, ask for heads and trimmings. Poach, steam, or bake the pieces for 20 minutes and you should be able to pick off a cup of meat. Canned salmon works fine in this recipe too. Buy sockeye (red) if you can afford it, pink if you want to save money.

---

1 small can (7¾ ounces) salmon, drained
***or* 1 cup flaked cooked salmon**
⅓ cup finely diced celery
2 tablespoons mayonnaise
1 teaspoon mustard
1 tablespoon minced fresh dill
***or* 1 teaspoon dried dill**
Tomato slices, cucumber slices, or capers, for garnish

Put the salmon in a bowl and break it into small flakes with a fork. Stir in the remaining ingredients. Spread about ¼ inch thick on room-temperature bagel halves and top with your choice of garnish.

Makes enough for 2 bagels

Best on rye and pumpernickel bagels.
I wouldn't put this on a sweet bagel.

ONE-FORK
TUNA SALAD

You probably already have your own favorite way to make tuna salad, but it's my book, so I'm going to tell you how I do it. However you make it, it's good on bagel halves, or for stuffing hollowed-out "tunnel bagels" (see page 108).

---

1 can (6⅛ ounces) oil-packed "chunk light" tuna
½ teaspoon spicy brown mustard
1 tablespoon mayonnaise (regular or reduced fat)
¼ cup finely diced celery

Using the lid of the can to hold the tuna in place, drain off about half of the oil. Before the fork ever touches the tuna, use it to scoop out the mustard and mayonnaise into a small bowl. (My wife scowls at the little mustard left behind in the mayo, but I don't care.) Now fork the tuna and the remaining oil out of the can into the bowl, add the celery, and mix everything up until it is to your liking — flakes coated with dressing or a homogeneous mash. Spread on room-temperature or toasted bagel halves.

Makes enough for 2 bagels

Good with any non-sweet bagel.

HAM AND CHEESE BAGEL

My wife went to a deli to pick up sandwiches for an impromptu picnic, and I asked her to get me a ham and cheese on rye. I guess, knowing her Jewish background, I should have been more specific. When they asked her "boiled ham or baked?" she was lost. Even those of us who grew up eating ham can get confused by all the different kinds available. Add in the endless variety of cheeses, and the permutations must run into the thousands. Here's my favorite. In a particulary well-stocked deli, I'd substitute cumin-flavored Leiden or Kumminost cheese for Edam.

---

1 bagel, split
Mustard
2 to 3 ounces sliced Black Forest-style ham
1 to 2 ounces sliced Edam cheese

Spread the bagel halves with mustard. Top one with ham and cheese and close to serve sandwich style, or divide the ham and cheese between the two halves and serve open face.

Variation:
For a double-decker sandwich, slice the bagel into thirds, then put the cheese and ham in separate layers.

Makes 1 sandwich

Best with rye or pumpernickel bagels.

DEVILED HAM

The old-fashioned word "deviled" means highly seasoned, and probably came from some phrase like "hot as the devil." It usually implies a lot of mustard, which we have here, and sometimes its cousin, horseradish, which is also present. You won't get flavor like this from a can.

¼ **pound cooked ham (about 1 cup)**
¼ **cup diced celery**
2 teaspoons capers or chopped dill pickle
2 tablespoons mayonnaise
1 tablespoon mustard
½ **teaspoon prepared horseradish**

Chop the ham, celery, and capers or pickles together finely (a food processor works well for this). Stir in the mayonnaise, mustard, and horseradish. Adjust the seasonings to taste.

Makes 1 cup, enough for 3 to 4 bagels

Best on pumpernickel, rye, onion, or plain bagels.

I don't eat liver sausage very often, but every now and then I get a taste for it. Its soft, spreadable texture is just right with the chewiness of a bagel. And it tastes really good with pickles.

---

1 bagel, split
Mustard
2 ounces liverwurst or Braunschweiger
Lettuce leaves or thinly sliced dill pickle

To serve open face, spread the bagel halves with a little mustard, then add a layer of liverwurst. Top with lettuce or pickles or both. This can also be assembled as a conventional sandwich.

Makes 1 bagel

Best on rye or pumpernickel bagels; good on any non-sweet bagel.

That staple of fast-food breakfasts, a ham and egg sandwich on English muffin, got me thinking about one of my mother-in-law's specialties, wurst (pronounced *voosht*) and eggs. She cooks kosher salami and eggs together in a skillet and serves them on a plate, but I see no reason why they can't go inside a bagel.

———————

1 tablespoon oil or chicken fat
2 or 3 slices (about 1 ounce) kosher salami
1 bagel, split
Mustard
1 egg
Salt and freshly ground pepper to taste

Heat the oil in a nonstick skillet over medium heat. Add the salami slices and cook until lightly browned on both sides. Meanwhile, spread the bagel halves with mustard and beat the egg with a pinch of salt and pepper. When the salami slices are done, drain them briefly on a paper towel and place them on the bottom bagel half. Add the egg to the skillet and tilt the pan so the egg runs out into a large, thin omelet. Reduce the heat to medium-low and cook until the egg is just set. With a spatula, fold up the omelet into a square that will fit on the bagel. Set it on top of the salami and top with the other bagel half, to eat sandwich style.

Makes 1 sandwich

Best on sesame, poppy, or plain bagels.

———————

REUBEN BAGEL

The original Reuben sandwich is made with sliced rye bread and is browned on a griddle. Here a rye or pumpernickel bagel stands in nicely for rye bread. I don't use the traditional Russian dressing because it tastes too sweet to me these days.

Mustard (optional)
¼ cup sauerkraut, well drained
2 ounces thinly sliced corned beef
1 ounce sliced Gruyère cheese

Slice a bagel and spread the halves with mustard. Top each half with corned beef, then sauerkraut, then cheese. Heat in a 350°F oven, under the broiler, or in a toaster oven until the cheese melts.

Makes 1 open bagel sandwich

Best on rye or pumpernickel bagels.
Don't do this on cinnamon raisin or any other sweet bagel.

HOT PASTRAMI

When I was younger, I would gleefully tackle the typical deli pastrami sandwich, with a quarter pound or more of sliced meat in an enormous pile that barely fit between two slices of bread. Now it just seems like too much meat (and besides, it would be totally unmanageable inside a bagel). So here's a saner version, with the ratio of meat to bread reversed. This will reheat well in the office microwave oven.

---

2 to 3 ounces sliced pastrami
1 bagel, split
Mustard
Dill pickle spears

Warm the pastrami in a double boiler, a Chinese-style steamer, or a microwave oven. Spread the bagel halves liberally with mustard, and lay on the pastrami as evenly as possible. Serve sandwich style, with pickle spears on the side.

Makes 1 sandwich

Best on rye, pumpernickel, sesame, or poppy bagels.

ROAST BEEF BAGEL

I love roast beef with horseradish. If you do too, try it on a bagel. For a brown-bag bagel sandwich that will make your co-workers drool with envy, spread the cheese just on the bagel bottom, then top with the rest of the ingredients. Use the onion garnish, or leave it off.

---

2 to 3 tablespoons cream cheese
½ teaspoon prepared horseradish
Salt to taste
2 to 3 ounces thinly sliced roast beef
Pickled Onion Rings (page 59), for garnish
1 bagel, split

Combine the cheese and horseradish and add salt to taste. To serve open-face, spread the cheese on both bagel halves and top with the meat. To make a sandwich, pile the fillings on the bottom half only, and cover with the top half. Garnish with onion rings if you like.

Makes 1 bagel

Best on pumpernickel, rye, or onion bagels.

If you've been to New Orleans, you've probably stopped at one of its Italian delis for a pungent, bulging muffuletta sandwich. This is its bagel brother. You can serve it open-face as described here, or in a hollowed-out bagel (see page 108) for brown-bagging.

---

1 cup mixed pickled vegetables (*giardiniera*), drained
¼ cup pitted green olives
1 clove garlic, minced
1 tablespoon olive oil
2 to 3 ounces thinly sliced salami (dry Italian or kosher style)
2 sesame or poppy seed bagels, split

Chop the vegetables and olives finely and combine them with the garlic and oil. Let stand a few hours to overnight for the flavors to blend. Toast the bagels if you like. Top each half with a thin layer of salami and a spread of the olive salad.

Makes 2 bagels

Best on sesame or poppy seed bagels.

LAMB WITH MINT RAITA

A *raita* is a cool Indian-style relish, usually based on yogurt. Try this any time you have leftover leg of lamb.

---

1 teaspoon oil
¼ teaspoon mustard seeds
⅛ teaspoon cumin seeds
½ cup plain yogurt
8 to 10 fresh mint leaves, shredded
1 teaspoon minced or grated ginger
Pinch of cayenne (optional)
4 bagels, split
½ pound thinly sliced cooked lamb

Heat the oil in a small skillet over medium heat. Add the seeds and cook until they sizzle and begin to pop. Remove the pan from the heat and let the seeds cool. Combine the yogurt, mint, and ginger, then stir in the seeds and their oil. Add a pinch of cayenne if you want a hotter flavor. Toast the bagel halves if you like, and top them with slices of lamb. Spoon the raita over the top.

Serves 4

Best with plain or poppy bagels.

CHOPPED LIVER

For countless generations, the ingredients for chopped liver have been cut up in a wooden bowl with a curved knife that rocks back and forth. My wife, who did not inherit her grandmother's curved knife, simply mashes everything together with the back of a fork. I use my food processor. If you use yours, remember it takes just a few quick pulses. Stop as soon as the mixture begins to smear on the bottom of the bowl. Otherwise you will end up with a texture more like pureed French mousse than Jewish chopped liver.

---

2 tablespoons oil or rendered chicken fat
1 medium onion, diced
½ pound chicken livers
¾ teaspoon kosher salt, or to taste
⅛ teaspoon freshly ground pepper, or to taste
1 hard-cooked egg, peeled

Heat the fat in a skillet over medium heat and saute the onion until it begins to color. Add the livers, salt, and pepper and cook, turning occasionally, until drops of blood appear on the tops of the livers and then disappear. (Cut open the largest piece; it should be barely pink in the center.) Remove the livers and onion with a slotted spoon and set them aside in a bowl to cool. When cool, chop the liver mixture and the egg together — by hand with a knife, in a meat grinder, or in a food processor — to a spreadable consistency. Taste for seasoning and adjust if necessary. Chill before serving. If the mixture seems too dry, stir in a little rendered chicken fat (fresh or from the skillet) or mayonnaise.

Makes 2 cups, enough for 4 to 6 bagels

Best on onion bagels.
Not good on sweet bagels.

BAGEL DOG, MY WAY

I've actually seen something in a supermarket freezer called a bagel dog; it's a frankfurter wrapped in bagel-like dough. I haven't gotten up the courage to try it. However, I have been known to split a hot dog and serve it up on top of half a bagel. You can do this with any similarly shaped fully cooked sausage — "dinner franks," turkey or chicken franks, knockwurst, bockwurst, Polish sausage, and so on.

---

2 frankfurters
1 bagel, split
Mustard
Sauerkraut or relish (optional)

Cut the sausages in half, then cut each half open lengthwise, almost splitting it in half but leaving the two halves connected by skin. Cook them in a nonstick skillet, starting cut side down, until they are heated through and lightly browned. Meanwhile, toast the bagel halves if you like and spread them with mustard and sauerkraut or relish. Lay two sausage halves side by side on top of each bagel half and eat open face.

Serves 2

Best on plain, poppy, or sesame bagels.

Pickled beets straight from the jar are my daughter's favorite vegetable. I like them too. Sweet and tart, somewhere between crunchy and tender, they are a handy ingredient to have on hand. As long as you don't mind pink stains on your cream cheese, they make a good bagel topping.

1 bagel, split
2 tablespoons cream cheese
¼ cup sliced pickled beets, well drained
Fresh dill, chives, or chervil, for garnish

Spread the bagel halves with cheese and top with a layer of overlapping beet slices. Garnish with something green.

Variation:
Beets and pickled herring are a great combination.

Makes 1 bagel

Whole roasted eggplant, either the large globe variety or the smaller Asian types, can be the base for all kinds of savory spreads. Three recipes follow, one Middle Eastern in origin, one Indian, one Chinese. They are all delicious on bagels, and they all start with the same procedure.

**1 pound eggplant (1 medium globe eggplant
or 3 to 4 small Asian types)
1 medium onion**

Puncture the eggplant once or twice with a toothpick and place it and the onion on a cookie sheet. Roast in a 400°F oven until the eggplant is thoroughly soft and the onion oozes juice, about 45 minutes. Remove from the oven. When it's cool enough to handle, split the eggplant lengthwise and carefully scrape all the flesh from the skin. Discard the skin and chop the flesh finely. Also discard the onion skin and any burned outer layers, and chop the rest of the onion finely. Combine the chopped eggplant and onion. The mixture is now ready for any of the three following recipes.

Makes 2 cups

BABA GANOUSH

I like saying baba ganoush almost as much as I like eating it. It's one of many terrific things you can do with eggplant. A Middle Eastern thing. To make any eggplant spread taste even better, roast the eggplant and onion over an open fire (on a grill) rather than in the oven. Scorching the skin adds a smoky flavor.

---

1 tablespoon olive oil
1 large clove garlic, minced
2 tablespoons sesame tahini
2 tablespoons lemon juice
½ teaspoon salt
Pinch of white pepper or cayenne
1 pound roasted eggplant mixture (see page 50)

Warm the oil and garlic gently in a wok or large skillet over low heat until the garlic is very fragrant but not browned. Turn off the heat and stir in the tahini, lemon juice, salt, and pepper. Stir in the eggplant mixture, correct the seasoning, and let cool completely before serving.

Makes 2 cups

Best on sesame, egg, plain, or salt bagels.

TANDOORI EGGPLANT

My favorite Indian restaurant roasts eggplant in a wood-fired clay oven called a *tandoor*. (If you've never had meats, vegetables, and breads roasted in a tandoor, put down the book and hurry to your nearest Indian restaurant. I'll wait.) I've tried to make this eggplant taste like tandoori eggplant, and I think I got pretty close.

---

2 tablespoons peanut or corn oil
1 large clove garlic, minced
1 tablespoon minced ginger
1 teaspoon garam masala (Indian spice mix; see page 113)
½ teaspoon turmeric
⅛ teaspoon cayenne
1 cup seeded and chopped tomato (fresh or canned)
½ teaspoon salt
1 pound roasted eggplant mixture (see page 50)

Heat the oil in a skillet over medium heat and cook the garlic and ginger until fragrant. Add the spices and cook 1 minute, then stir in the tomato and salt. Simmer until the tomato juice is nearly gone, then turn off the heat and stir in the eggplant mixture. Taste for seasoning and let cool to lukewarm or room temperature before spreading on warm toasted bagels.

Makes 2 cups

Chinese cooks know their eggplant and they know how to balance flavors. This spread has a typically Chinese blend of sweet, sour, salty, and hot elements. Feel free to adjust the balance to your personal taste.

---

2 tablespoons peanut or corn oil
½ cup chopped green onion
1 tablespoon minced ginger
Pinch of hot pepper flakes
2 tablespoons soy sauce
2 teaspoons Chinese Chekiang rice vinegar or balsamic vinegar
½ teaspoon sugar
1 pound roasted eggplant mixture (see page 50)

Heat the oil in a wok or skillet over medium heat and cook the green onion and ginger until fragrant. Add the pepper flakes, soy sauce, vinegar, and sugar and stir just until the sugar dissolves. Turn off the heat and stir in the eggplant mixture. Taste for seasoning and adjust to your taste. Serve lukewarm or at room temperature on warm or toasted bagels.

Makes 2 cups

REAL GARLIC BAGELS

I know, I know, you can buy garlic bagels. So why a recipe? Because these bagels are totally different. They're a bagel version of *bruschetta*, the original, incredibly delicious garlic bread of central Italy. Use the best olive oil you can get your hands on — the kind that seems too good even for salad dressing. If you're grilling dinner, toast some bagels on the grill just before you start cooking, and enjoy these as an appetizer.

_____

1 bagel, split
1 clove garlic, peeled
1 tablespoon (approximately) extra virgin olive oil
Salt and pepper

Toast the bagel in the toaster or under the broiler. Impale the garlic on a fork. While the bagel is still hot from toasting, rub the cut surface with the garlic; the more you rub on, the stronger the flavor. Drizzle or brush the surface with oil — again, as much or as little as you like. Sprinkle with a little salt (unless it's a salt bagel) and pepper and eat immediately, preferably with a glass of wine.

Makes 1 bagel

Best on plain, poppy seed, or salt bagels.

_____

TOMATO-BASIL GARLIC BAGEL

Bruschetta, wonderful by itself, soars to new heights when crowned with ripe summer tomatoes and shreds of basil.

---

1 tablespoon extra virgin olive oil
¼ cup seeded and diced ripe tomato
2 tablespoons shredded basil leaves
Pinch of salt
1 bagel, split
1 clove garlic, peeled

Combine the oil, tomato, basil, and salt and let the mixture stand 15 minutes. Toast the bagel in the toaster or under the broiler. Impale the garlic on a fork. While the bagel is still hot from toasting, rub the cut surface with the garlic. Spoon the tomato mixture on top. Eat at once.

Makes 1 bagel

ROASTED GARLIC

Roasted garlic tastes completely different from garlic that is chopped or minced before cooking. It is mellow and sweet. Just squeeze some out of its papery skin, mash it with a fork, and mix in a little olive oil for a delicious spread to go on bagels alone or under meats. A roasted head of garlic will keep for a week or more in the refrigerator, so whenever you see nice-looking garlic, buy several extra heads and roast them.

Whole, firm heads of garlic
Olive oil
Salt and freshly ground pepper to taste

Preheat the oven to 375°F. Slice off the top quarter or so of each head of garlic to expose the tops of most of the cloves. Place the heads cut side up in a deep covered casserole and drizzle them with a little oil. Cover and bake until the exposed cloves are soft and golden brown, 45 minutes to an hour. Let cool, then squeeze out as many cloves as you need into a bowl. Mash them with a fork and work in a few drops of oil. Season to taste with salt and pepper.

ROASTED PEPPER CHEESE SPREAD

Sweet peppers and salty feta cheese remind me of Greece and an exuberant Zorba-type fellow we met there. Eftikes (that was his name) would probably not approve of my mixing feta with cream cheese, but for me a little feta goes a long way. You may find even my mixture too assertive; adjust the ratio of cheeses to suit your taste. Please don't take your roasted peppers from a jar. This spread needs the sweetness of a freshly roasted pepper. I developed this recipe on the same day I was testing the "refried" beans on page 69. And you know what? The two are very good together, on the same bagel.

---

1 sweet pepper (red, orange, or yellow)
1 ounce feta cheese (about a 1-inch cube), well drained
3 ounces cream cheese
⅛ teaspoon dried oregano, crumbled

Roast and peel the pepper (see page 115). Finely dice enough to give you 2 to 3 tablespoons; save the rest for another use. Drain well. Mash the feta well in a bowl with the back of a fork. Add the cream cheese and combine with a rubber spatula. Add the peppers and oregano and mix thoroughly.

Makes ¾ cup, enough for 6 to 8 bagels

Best on sesame, poppy, and other "plain vanilla" type bagels.

Now for the sophisticates among us, an *haute cuisine* bagel spread. The French would call this a *confit*, but onion marmalade really says it all: it's a little sweet, more than a little tart, and easily spreadable. It takes a bit of time to make, but it's worth it, and the recipe makes a lot. Try it alone or over cream cheese. Serve it to someone special.

1½ pounds red or yellow onions
3 tablespoons olive oil
1 cup Zinfandel or other dry red wine
4 tablespoons red wine vinegar or raspberry vinegar
2 teaspoons honey

Slice the onions crosswise as thinly as possible. Heat the oil in a heavy covered casserole or skillet over medium heat. Add the onions, cover, and cook until they begin to soften, about 5 minutes. Add the wine, vinegar, and honey and bring to a boil. Reduce the heat to as low as possible, replace the cover, and cook until the onions are quite soft, 1 to 2 hours. Remove the cover, turn up the heat and cook, stirring, until the liquid is nearly evaporated. Spoon into clean jars, cover, and refrigerate up to 2 weeks.

Makes 2 pints

PICKLED ONION RINGS

I used to love raw onions, but now they don't sit so very well. By pickling an onion you change whatever it is that stomachs like mine — and many others — don't like. Even if you can eat raw onions with abandon, you should try them pickled. They taste great alone and enhance other toppings, from plain cream cheese to lox, hummus, salmon or tuna salad, herring, turkey...but probably not peanut butter and jelly.

Red onions look best, but sometimes they're expensive. Use whatever kind of onion is sweetest and most reasonably priced. (White and yellow onions turn pink if you add a little liquid from a jar of pickled beets.)

---

1 medium onion
Boiling water
¼ teaspoon salt
6 peppercorns
½ cup rice or cider vinegar (approximately)
½ cup water (approximately)

Peel the onion and slice it into rings about ⅛ inch thick. Place the rings in a bowl and cover them with boiling water. After 5 minutes, drain in a colander and rinse with cold water. Stuff the rings into a pint glass jar and sprinkle in the salt and peppercorns. Add equal parts vinegar and water, enough to cover the onion. Refrigerate overnight; the onions will keep for weeks in the refrigerator.

Makes 1 pint

GARLIC AND HERB CHEESE

Do you like Boursin and other imported herbed cheeses? Do you know you can make a very good, cheaper version at home? I tried this recipe using fresh goat cheese in place of half the cream cheese, but it was hard to taste the difference through the garlic and herbs, so it's probably not worth the extra cost.

---

1 small clove garlic
1 tablespoon chopped mild herbs (parsley, chives, chervil, dill, or a blend)
1 teaspoon lemon zest, grated or removed in strips with a peeler
6 ounces cream cheese
Pinch of pepper

Blanch the garlic in a small pot of boiling water for 1 minute; drop it into cold water to cool. Peel the clove and trim off the root end. Chop the garlic, herbs, and lemon zest together as finely as possible. Beat the cheese with a spoon or rubber spatula until it's soft and light. Stir in the garlic-herb mixture and pepper to taste. Pack the mixture into a small container, cover it tightly, and refrigerate 1 hour to 7 days.

Makes enough for 6 to 8 bagels

Best on plain, sesame, or poppy seed bagels.
Not good on raisin or other sweet bagels.

CREAM CHEESE AND JELLY

This is one that the kids really like and, better yet, one they can make themselves. It couldn't be simpler.

---

1 ounce cream cheese
1 bagel, split
Jam or jelly

Toast the bagel if you like. Spread a layer of cream cheese on each half and top with your favorite jam or jelly. Spread it thick or thin depending on your tastes and your mood. For really small children, it's best to make this as a closed sandwich — and keep them off the good furniture until they're done.

Makes 1 bagel

Best on plain, seeded, or sweet bagels.

COTTAGE CHEESE AND FRUIT

No, cottage cheese is not as rich in taste as cream cheese, but it does allow you to save most of your fat allowance for other foods. Something about cottage cheese — maybe years of seeing it as the centerpiece of "dieter's special" plates — suggests fruit as a partner. Try pineapple (preferably fresh), mango, pears, apples, grapes, orange sections, strawberries or other berries, or whatever fruit looks good in the market.

---

1 bagel, split and toasted
½ cup cottage cheese
¼ cup diced fresh fruit

If the bagel has a large hole, use a couple of whole berries or other nice pieces of fruit to plug it. Spread the cheese liberally on the bagel halves, then top with fruit.

Makes 1 bagel

Best on plain, egg, or raisin bagels.
Onion, garlic, and rye bagels are okay if you skip the fruit.

LEMON CURD

Thick, smooth, tart-sweet lemon curd is incredibly delicious, no matter what you put it on. If you're not lucky enough to know a home canner who likes to make it and give it away, look for it near the imported jams and marmalades in the supermarket. Try it plain or with a little cream cheese.

---

1 bagel, split
1 tablespoon cream cheese (optional)
2 tablespoons lemon curd

Toast or warm the bagel halves. Spread on a little cream cheese if you like, then add a liberal layer of lemon curd.

Chocolate Variation:
Forget the cream cheese. Sprinkle 2 teaspoons of grated bittersweet chocolate on each *hot* bagel half. Let it melt, then add the lemon curd. Heavenly!

Best on raisin or other fruit-studded bagels.
Also good on whole grain or multigrain bagels.

PROSCIUTTO AND FRUIT

The Italians discovered long ago that the intense flavor of prosciutto, a dry-cured, unsmoked ham, marries beautifully with sweet, juicy fruit. They often pair it with fresh cantaloupe or honeydew melon, but peaches, nectarines, pears, and figs all work well. Use whichever fruit looks, smells, and tastes best when you shop. I don't think this needs cream cheese, but a very thin spread wouldn't hurt.

---

1 ounce thinly sliced prosciutto
1 bagel, split
2 ounces sweet fruit

Trim any excess fat from the prosciutto and cut it into several pieces to fit on the bagel halves. Cut the fruit (peeled first if necessary) into thick slices or wedges and arrange them on top, overlapping slightly. Serve immediately.

Makes 1 bagel

Best on sesame, poppy, or egg bagels.

Some blue cheeses, such as Gorgonzola and Cambozola, are soft and smooth enough to spread. Most, however, are crumbly and tend to fall apart into pebble-sized pieces which fall off bagels. It's best to mix the blue cheese into cream cheese, which also softens the flavor.

---

2 ounces cream cheese
2 ounces crumbled blue cheese (about ¼ cup)
2 tablespoons finely chopped walnuts or pecans (optional)
4 to 6 bagels, split
1 ripe but firm pear

Beat the cream cheese in a bowl until light. Stir in the blue cheese and nuts and mix until the blue cheese is evenly distributed but not totally dissolved. Spread on warm or room-temperature bagel halves. Halve and core the pear and peel it if you like. Cut it into thin wedges and arrange them on top of the cheese.

Makes 4 to 6 bagels

AVOCADO AND CRAB BAGEL

Californians have always loved avocados. Avocado and shellfish were already old friends in southern California back when there were more orange trees than people. It's still a favorite combination.

---

1 large or 2 small ripe avocados, halved and pitted
½ teaspoon lemon juice, or to taste
Salt to taste
Bottled green chile salsa (optional)
2 bagels, split
4 cherry tomatoes (optional)
1 cup cooked crabmeat

Scoop out the avocado and mash the flesh. Add the lemon juice, salt, and as much salsa as you like. Spread the avocado on the bagel halves (use cherry tomatoes as hole pluggers, if needed) and arrange the crab on top. Drizzle on a little more salsa if you like.

Variation:
You can use tiny cooked shrimp in place of crab.

Makes 2 bagels

Best with sesame, plain, or poppy bagels.

CALIFORNIA SALAD BAGEL

When people want to make fun of California cuisine, they point to its salads of "baby" lettuces and greens with names like arugula, frisée, and radicchio (topped, of course, with baked goat cheese). But have you tasted one of those salads? They're worth the trip. Now you can buy bags of assorted greens, already washed, in many supermarkets. If you don't want to make your own dressing, use a bottled oil and vinegar dressing.

---

1 scant teaspoon balsamic vinegar
Pinch of salt and pepper
1 tablespoon extra virgin olive oil
A handful of mixed salad greens
4 bagels, split
2 ounces goat cheese, at room temperature
Tiny red or yellow pear tomatoes, sliced (optional)

In a small bowl, stir the vinegar, salt, and pepper together, then stir in the oil. Add the greens and toss. Toast the bagel bottoms. While they're still hot, spread 1 tablespoon of cheese on each. Heap salad on top, then add a few tomato slices and the bagel tops.

Serves 4

Best on plain or seeded bagels.
Not good on sweet bagels.

TROPICAL AVOCADO SALAD

I know salad on a bagel sounds strange at first, but this is really good. It's based on one of my favorite salads. I tried it first with slices of avocado, but the little cubes of jicama kept sliding off. (The combination tasted so good I kept picking them up and putting them back on top.) The next time, I mashed the avocado — same great taste but much more structurally stable. A great light lunch.

---

1 pink grapefruit
1 medium-size ripe avocado, halved and pitted
Salt, to taste
¼ cup peeled and finely diced jicama (see page 113)

Slice off the top and bottom of the grapefruit. Cut away the skin and white pith all around. Working over a bowl to catch the juices, cut carefully between the membranes to get out the skinless sections. If the sections are very thick, cut each one into two skinny sections. Scoop out the avocado and mash it. Add salt to taste. Spread the avocado on bagel halves and sprinkle on some jicama cubes, pressing them in lightly so they don't fall off. Top with a few grapefruit sections.

Makes enough for 2 bagels

Best on whole wheat, multigrain, and salt bagels.
Not for onion and garlic bagels.

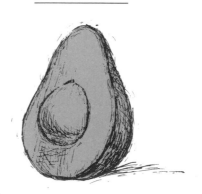

Why not? Refried beans are great for topping tortillas, filling burritos, as a dip for tortilla chips — and as a bagel spread. I cook my beans without the usual lard or vegetable oil. There's no question that the extra fat in real refried beans adds a richer flavor and texture, but I discovered years ago that you can get awfully close by simply mashing the beans and cooking them down in their own broth. I like to save the fat for where it really counts — the cheese on top.

---

2 cups cooked black or pinto beans, with their broth
(or a 15-ounce can)
½ small onion, grated (about ¼ cup)
1 clove garlic, minced
Hot pepper sauce, to taste
Grated cheese (Parmesan, Romano, asiago, or dry jack)

Combine the beans, broth, onion, garlic, and a dash of pepper sauce in a cast-iron skillet. Bring to a boil slowly while mashing the beans with a potato masher. Turn the heat to low and simmer, stirring occasionally, until the mixture is thick and dry enough to hold its shape, 20 to 30 minutes. Stir and scrape the pan frequently in the last few minutes to keep the beans from scorching. Taste for seasoning and adjust if necessary. Spread on toasted bagel halves and top each with a teaspoon or so of grated cheese.

Variation:
Use a thinner spread of beans and add a little Roasted Pepper Cheese Spread (page 57) on top instead of grated cheese.

Makes 1½ cups, enough for 3 or 4 bagels

Best on plain or seeded bagels.
Not good on sweet bagels.

My mother has always had a great repertoire of dishes based on hard-boiled eggs, often with strong flavors like olives and bacon in supporting roles. Here the roles are reversed. A bit of egg, and some mushrooms, stretch and soften the flavor of an olive spread.

⅓ cup stuffed green olives
2 slices bacon, cooked crisp and drained
1 hard-boiled egg
3 medium mushrooms, wiped clean

Combine all the ingredients in a food processor and chop to a spreadable but still slightly chunky texture.

Vegetarian variation:
Omit the bacon. Toast 1 tablespoon of pine nuts in the oven or in a skillet and chop them by hand. Stir them into the chopped mixture.

Makes ¾ cup, enough for 4 to 6 bagels

Best on toasted onion, garlic, or other plain-type bagels.
Use a whole olive to plug the bagel hole, if you like.
Not good on sweet bagels.

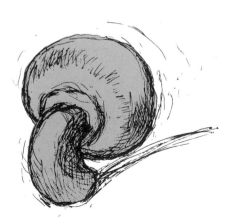

EGG SALAD

Egg salad is an opportunity for personal expression. Some folks like it very simple. Others load it with crunch and assertive flavors. What makes egg salad exciting for me is a strong salty accent. Here I've used anchovy. Sometimes I like to put in capers or finely chopped olives or pickles. If you go for crunch, try adding chopped celery, sweet pepper, or green or yellow onion. Whatever you like best is what you should put in.

---

1 hard-cooked egg
2 teaspoons mayonnaise
¼ teaspoon mustard
1 anchovy filet, minced, *or* ¼ teaspoon anchovy paste
Salt and freshly ground pepper to taste

Separate the egg white and yolk. Mash the yolk in a bowl with the mayonnaise, mustard, and anchovy. Chop the white finely and stir it in. Season to taste and spread on toasted bagel halves.

Makes 1 bagel

Good on any not-sweet bagel.

PEANUT BUTTER AND MUSTARD

One of my first culinary creations, at about age 5, was a peanut butter and mustard sandwich on rye bread. I enjoyed that combination for years, until a friend told me that peanut butter on rye bread was weird (I didn't dare tell him about the mustard). Older, presumably wiser, and less concerned with what other people think, I recently tried to recapture this flavor from my youth, but it just didn't taste right. Then it dawned on me that the peanut butter Mom bought in those days was sweeter than the kind I like today. So I added some sugar, and it was just right. (If your peanut butter brand is sweetened, try this first without the added sugar.)

---

1 rye bagel, split
1 teaspoon "spicy brown" or yellow mustard
2 tablespoons peanut butter
¼ teaspoon sugar

Toast the bagel if you like. Spread each half with mustard, then with peanut butter. Sprinkle a little sugar evenly over the top and eat warm or at room temperature. Made sandwich-style, this is a good bag lunch. Honest.

Makes 1 bagel

Also good on pumpernickel, plain, and sesame bagels.

PEANUT BUTTER AND JELLY

Peanut butter and jelly is not as simple as it might seem. There are lots of decisions to make. Look at the options just in peanut butter: Smooth or chunky? Regular or unsalted? All-natural or processed so it doesn't separate? Sweetened or not? And now there are reduced-fat versions. And jelly! Do you use actual jelly (not the best choice — it tends to fall off) or jam, preserves, fancy imported *confitures*, 100-percent-fruit spreads? And which fruit? Then there's the bagel. What kind? And should it be toasted or not? All I can say is trust your instincts. Fact is, any bagel (with the possible exception of green olive) tastes good toasted and topped with peanut butter and something sweet. Use a peanut butter that you feel good about and a fruit spread that appeals to you. If you find you like peanut butter and orange marmalade on an onion bagel, don't let anyone talk you out of it. If you feel like branching out to other nut butters such as almond, cashew, or hazelnut, go for it (see page 74).

---

1 bagel
1 to 2 tablespoons peanut butter
1 to 2 tablespoons jam or preserves

Split and toast the bagel and spread each half with peanut butter, then jam. Enjoy open-faced. Or skip the toasting and prepare the bagel sandwich style for brown-bagging.

Makes 1 bagel

Peanuts aren't the only nuts that can be ground into butter. Rich and delicious cashew and almond butters are fairly common at health-food stores; hazelnut (filbert) butter is a little harder to find but is equally scrumptious. Try any of them on bagels, with or without jam. I particularly like peach or apricot jam with almond butter, and blackberry or raspberry jam with cashew butter.

To make your own nut butter at home, first toast the nuts (raw cashews, blanched almonds, whole raw hazelnuts) in a 350°F oven until light brown. Rub the skins off the hazelnuts with a towel after toasting. Chop the nuts in a food processor, stopping to scrape down the sides of the bowl occasionally, until you get a smooth paste. This can take several minutes. Salt to taste and store in a jar in the refrigerator or at room temperature.

---

1 bagel, split and toasted
1 to 2 tablespoons nut butter
1 to 2 tablespoons jam

Spread the bagels as thickly as you like with nut butter,
then with jam.

Makes 1 bagel

HUMMUS

This chick-pea and tahini spread is smooth, garlicky, and delicious. It's an intriguing taste of the Middle East and a great alternative to cream cheese. Chick-peas, garbanzo beans, and ceci are all the same bean; what you call them depends on where you live.

---

1 can (15 ounces) garbanzo beans
3 tablespoons roasted sesame tahini
2 cloves garlic, peeled
1 teaspoon kosher salt
¼ teaspoon paprika (sweet or hot)
¼ cup fresh lemon juice

Drain the garbanzos (save the juice). Combine the beans, tahini, garlic, salt, paprika, and lemon juice in a food processor or blender and blend to a smooth paste. Thin with a little bean juice if necessary to achieve a consistency thicker than mayonnaise but easily spreadable. Let rest 1 hour or more for the best flavor, or cover and refrigerate up to 2 days.

Makes 2 cups

BAGEL PIZZA

Since bagels are now as American as pizza, let's enjoy them that way. Pizza-style sauce, toppings, and cheese provide plenty of flavor, so you may as well start with plain bagels. (Some topping combinations might be even better on onion or garlic bagels.) Remember that the sauce needs to be thick enough to spread on the bagel without making it soggy. You might try bottled dried tomato "pesto" as an alternative.

½ teaspoon minced garlic
Pinch of coarse salt
1 tablespoon tomato paste
1 teaspoon olive oil
Pinch of dried oregano
Pepper, to taste
2 bagels, split
2 ounces sliced or coarsely grated mozzarella
1 tablespoon grated Parmesan cheese
Pizza toppings (see next page)

In a small bowl, mash the garlic and salt together with the back of a spoon. Stir in the tomato paste, oil, oregano, and pepper. Spread a teaspoon or so of this sauce on each bagel half, add the cheeses, and finish with your choice of toppings. Broil until the cheese is melted and beginning to brown. Serve as is or cut each half into halves or wedges.

Serves 2 to 4

You can top your bagel pizzas with any of your favorite pizza toppings. Here are a few of my favorites. Use just one, or mix and match.

---

1. Thinly sliced mushrooms.

2. Sliced and slivered dry salami or other ready-to-eat sausage.

3. Eggplant — roasted, peeled, and chopped (page 50) or sliced and cooked as for an Italian Bagel (page 83).

4. Sliced and lightly sauteed leeks or green onions.

5. Precooked slices of Italian sausage.

6. Leftover cooked chicken or turkey.

7. Artichoke hearts and slivers of prosciutto.

Think of it as a Mexican bagel pizza. Or a bagel quesadilla. Whatever you call it, what you've got is chile and cheese — an all-time favorite flavor combination. If you want, you can replace the Monterey jack with domestic munster, good mozzarella, or a fresh Mexican-style cheese. Buy your chiles in a can or roast and peel your own (see page 115). Use the long green Anaheim (like the one in the can) or the hotter, more triangular *chile poblano*, a.k.a. *chile pasilla*.

---

1 whole roasted and peeled green chile
1 bagel, split
1 ounce (approximately) Monterey jack cheese

Preheat the oven to 350° to 400°F. Slit the chile open lengthwise and remove the stem and any seeds. Cut the chile into narrow strips about 2 inches long. Arrange them in a loose pile on each bagel half, top with a slice of cheese, and bake on a cookie sheet until the cheese melts. Serve immediately.

Makes 1 bagel

Best on plain, poppy, or sesame bagels.

CHILE-CHEESE VARIATIONS

You can have a lot of fun adding flavors to a chile and cheese bagel. Be adventurous. Here are a few ideas to get you started.

---

1. If your chiles are not especially hot, add a dab of your favorite chile salsa.

2. Add a spoonful of lightly cooked corn kernels along with the chiles.

3. Top the chiles with thinly sliced mushrooms.

4. Add shredded cooked chicken on top of the chiles and under the cheese.

5. Add slices of sauteed onion.

6. If you roast and peel your own chiles, put a whole or halved onion alongside them and roast until soft. Discard the charred skin and surface; the rest will be sweet and soft. Add a slice, under the cheese.

7. Mix the chile strips into eggs (see Scrambled Egg and Cheese, page 25).

SATAY-STYLE CHICKEN BAGEL

When I visited Singapore last summer, I ate prodigious amounts of mouthwatering chicken satay. This version is easy to make at home.

1 boneless chicken breast
1 tablespoon oil
½ teaspoon ground coriander
¼ teaspoon turmeric
Pinch of salt
2 slices ginger
1 clove garlic
1 or 2 bagels, split
2 tablespoons Spicy Peanut Sauce (opposite)

Moisten the chicken breast with a few drops of oil and place it between two layers of waxed paper or inside a clean produce bag. Pound with a mallet, a champagne bottle, or the side of a cleaver until the breast is evenly flattened to about ⅛ inch thick. Place it in a shallow bowl, drizzle with the oil, and sprinkle in the coriander, turmeric, and salt. Slap the ginger and garlic with the side of a knife to flatten them slightly and add them to the bowl. Marinate 30 minutes to overnight in the refrigerator.

Divide the chicken into 2 roughly equal portions. Heat a nonstick skillet over medium-high heat and cook the chicken just until springy and opaque, about 2 minutes per side. Meanwhile, toast the bagel halves and spread each with 1 tablespoon of peanut sauce. Top with the chicken slices. Serve open face or sandwich style.

Serves 2

Best on sesame or egg bagels.

SPICY PEANUT SAUCE

This sauce is a simplified version of the satay sauces popular all over Southeast Asia. It's fine as is for a bagel spread, and it's wonderful with thinly sliced cooked meats.

---

1 tablespoon oil
1 tablespoon *each* minced garlic and ginger
2 tablespoons minced shallot or onion
½ to 1 teaspoon crushed red pepper
2 tablespoons dried unsweetened coconut flakes
1 tablespoon sugar
1 tablespoon soy sauce
1 tablespoon lemon or lime juice
2 tablespoons coconut milk or water
⅓ cup peanut butter

Combine the oil, garlic, ginger, and shallot in a small skillet and cook over low heat until the shallot is translucent. Add the pepper flakes and coconut and cook until the chile fragrance comes out. Sprinkle in the sugar, then stir in the soy sauce, lemon juice, and coconut milk. Remove from the heat and stir in the peanut butter. Taste for seasoning and adjust if necessary. Refrigerate if keeping overnight, but bring back to room temperature or warmer before serving. To serve, spread on toasted bagel halves. Top, if desired, with chicken satay (opposite) or beef, lamb, pork, or turkey breast, sliced thinly across the grain and seasoned and cooked satay-style.

Makes a scant ½ cup

Here's a classy dish that's easy to make, because someone else does the cooking. Cantonese-style roast duck is the secret weapon of many a smart cook. If you have a Chinatown nearby, look for a Cantonese restaurant (or better still, a take-out shop) with mahogany-colored roast ducks hanging in the window.

---

4 tablespoons hoisin sauce
½ teaspoon Chinese or Japanese sesame oil
Pinch of sugar
Soy sauce to taste
½ a Chinese-style roast duck, not cut up
4 sesame seed bagels, split
Watercress, baby mustard, or arugula leaves (optional)

Combine the hoisin sauce, sesame oil, and sugar in a small bowl; season to taste with soy sauce. Carve the meat from the duck in large sections, with the skin attached. Cut the meat crosswise into slices with skin (if the fat layer under the skin is especially thick, remove it and just include strips of the browned outer skin). Spread each bagel half with a little sauce and top with duck slices. Garnish with greens.

Serves 4

Best on sesame seed bagels.

ITALIAN BAGEL

I don't think bagels are really hot items in Italy...yet. When the Italians do discover bagels, I think this is one way they are going to want to eat them. And even if they don't, we can.

———————————

1 eggplant (about ¾ pound)
Salt
2 tablespoons olive oil
2 bagels, split
¼ cup shredded fresh basil leaves
4 ounces mozzarella (preferably fresh), sliced a little less
than ¼-inch thick
Freshly ground black pepper
1 ripe tomato, halved, seeded, and finely diced

Slice the eggplant crosswise into ¼-inch-thick rounds. Lay the slices on a cookie sheet or broiler pan, sprinkle lightly with salt, and brush the tops with olive oil. Broil 2 to 3 inches from the heat until nicely browned, about 5 minutes. Turn the slices over and brush the tops with oil; rearrange the slices on the pan if necessary so they cook evenly. Broil on the second side until all the slices are tender. Brush with a little more oil as they come out of the oven.

Select 4 slices as close as possible to the size of your bagels. (Save the rest in the refrigerator for another day. They are delicious hot, cold, or anywhere in between.) Top each bagel half with a slice of eggplant and a sprinkling of basil. Add a layer of cheese and a bit of pepper and put them back under the broiler until the cheese melts and begins to brown, about 3 minutes.
Top with a spoonful of tomato.

Makes 2 bagels

Best on plain or sesame bagels.

———————————

The unusual Norwegian goat cheese called *gjetost* includes the whey that is normally discarded in the cheesemaking process. They boil down the whey until it caramelizes, then blend it back into fresh goat cheese to produce a firm, dense block with a flavor somewhere between Hershey's caramels and peanut butter, plus a bit of sour tang. Look for it in small red boxes in well-stocked cheese shops. It's one of those love-it-or-hate-it foods; ask for a taste if you're not sure. If gjetost is not to your taste, try this with Gruyère, Fontina, or other nutty-tasting cheeses.

This is one of my favorite toppings for whole wheat and "granola" bagels — the multi-grain kind with sunflower seeds and other wholesome goodies.

---

1 ounce gjetost, sliced
1 tart green apple, cored and sliced
2 bagels, split

Remove the apple and cheese from the refrigerator a half hour ahead of time to let them come back toward room temperature. Toast the bagels or warm them in the oven. As soon as they come out, lay on the cheese and top with apple slices.

Makes 2 bagels

Best on whole wheat and multi-grain bagels.
Also good on sesame, poppy, egg, or plain bagels.

I think "Hawaiian Pizza," that pizza-chain standard, is a silly idea. But strip away the mozzarella, tomato sauce, and oregano and you are left with a good flavor combination — sweet-salty ham and sweet-tart pineapple. It makes a fine topping for bagels. (Thin slices of fresh pineapple are very good in place of canned.) I wonder if this will catch on in Honolulu.

---

1 bagel, split
1 tablespoon cream cheese (optional)
1 to 2 ounces sliced deli ham or Canadian bacon
2 canned pineapple rings, drained

Toast the bagel halves, if you like. Spread each half with a thin layer of cheese, add a slice of ham, and top with a ring of pineapple.

Variation:
Broil the pineapple slices first until lightly browned.

Makes 1 bagel

Best on sesame, poppy, or egg bagels.
The broiled variation is also good on onion bagels.

Denmark's most famous dish is smørrebrød, artfully arranged open-face sandwiches on buttered bread. The breads for smørrebrød are sliced very thin, so they must be dense and sturdy — like bagels. Now, I know these aren't authentic, but they taste great, and an assortment of these smørrebrød-like sandwiches on a big platter makes for an unusual and satisfying lunch. Make sandwiches with various meats, smoked or cured fish, cheeses, and vegetables on thin slices of white, rye, and pumpernickel bagel. Take the time to make the sandwiches decorative.

---

1 bagel
2 tablespoons softened unsalted butter
or **3 to 4 tablespoons cream cheese**
Smørrebrød toppings (see next page)

Slice the bagel into 4 even slices. If you have one of the new-fangled bagel holders that allow you to cut various thicknesses, you should have no problem. Otherwise, getting even slices will test your knife skills. If you're slicing with a knife, try laying the bagel between two thick wooden chopsticks and let the knife ride along the chopsticks to make even slices about ¼ inch thick. (This may take a little practice.) Spread the slices generously with butter or cream cheese, then top with the smørrebrød topping of your choice.

Makes 4 bagel smørrebrød

SMØRREBRØD TOPPINGS

1. *Sardine and cucumber:* Peel and thinly slice ½ a medium cucumber. Arrange the slices, overlapped, on 4 thin slices of pumpernickel bagel. Open a can (3¾ ounces) of sardines in mustard or tomato sauce and arrange the sardine pieces in an attractive pattern on top.

2. *Pickled beets and pickled herring:* Arrange slices of well-drained pickled beets in a single layer; top with sliced pickled herring. Garnish with pickled onions (page 59) or a sprig of dill.

3. *Smoked fish:* Spread the horseradish-flavored cream cheese on page 44 on thin slices of rye or pumpernickel bagel. Top with thick slices of hot-smoked fish and curls of lemon peel.

4. *Salami and olives:* Arrange thin slices of Italian or kosher salami in a circle. Top with a ring of sliced stuffed olives.

5. *Liver pâté:* Use slices of coarse country-style pâté, or spread the smooth style in a thick layer. (Or use the Chopped Liver on page 47.) Garnish with cornichons, sliced nearly to the end and fanned out.

6. *New potatoes and bacon:* Arrange slices of boiled red potatoes in an overlapping ring on bagel slices. Slice or crumble crisp bacon and scatter it on top of the potatoes. Garnish with chopped chives.

7. *Cheese:* Use a flavorful semihard cheese that slices easily, such as Danish Havarti, Esrom, Dutch Edam, or Leiden. Garnish with thinly sliced radishes.

8. *Celery vinaigrette:* Braise celery hearts until tender. Marinate in mustard vinaigrette. Cover bagel slices with slices of celery and top with a couple of rolled-up thin slices of ham.

GREEK BAGEL

I never saw a bagel in Greece, but I ate countless summer salads of ripe tomatoes, feta, and cucumbers. I hope my Greek hosts, who always liked a good laugh, won't mind this innovation. Getting everything to stay on a bagel requires cutting thinner slices than you would ever find served on a plate in a *taverna*.

¼ of a medium cucumber
1 small tomato
1 bagel, split
Kalamata or other large black olives
1 to 2 ounces feta cheese
1 teaspoon extra virgin olive oil
Pinch of dried oregano leaves, crumbled
Freshly ground pepper to taste

Peel the cucumber if you like and cut about a dozen very thin slices. Cut the tomato in half through the stem end and slice one half crosswise as thinly as you can. Toast the bagel halves and let them cool. Put an olive in the center of each half as a hole plugger, then slice the feta thinly and carefully arrange it on the two halves. Top each with a layer of slightly overlapped cucumber slices, then tomato slices. Drizzle with a tiny bit of oil and top with oregano and pepper. Serve with more olives on the side.

Makes 1 bagel

Best on sesame, poppy, or plain bagels.

Romesco is a thick paste of red peppers, nuts, garlic, and olive oil which Spanish and Catalán cooks use as a sauce for meats and vegetables. I've always liked mopping up the last bits with bread, so I wasn't surprised to discover it tastes great on bagels. Try it plain or topped with cold chicken, turkey, or fish. Almonds or hazelnuts are traditional in Romesco, but I also like pistachios.

---

2 cloves garlic
¼ teaspoon salt
¼ cup blanched almonds or unsalted pistachio meats
½ large roasted and peeled red pepper (see page 115)
1 tablespoon extra virgin olive oil
1 teaspoon lemon juice, or to taste
White pepper or cayenne to taste

Traditional method: Pound the garlic and salt to a paste in a mortar, then add the nuts and grind fine. Add the red pepper and mash to a paste, then stir in the oil, lemon juice, and any juices from the red pepper. Season to taste.

Easy method: Combine everything in a blender or food processor and process to a puree, stopping to scrape down the sides as necessary.

Makes ½ cup, enough for 4 to 6 bagels

Best on plain, seeded, or onion bagels.

CHICKEN SHIITAKE SALAD

Chicken salad is always good on bagels. This one has a Japanese accent. It was inspired by a recipe in *Japanese Cooking: A Simple Art* by Shizuo Tsuji. Tsuji used a pureed tofu dressing instead of mayonnaise and, of course, he didn't serve it on bagels.

---

4 dried shiitake mushrooms
1 tablespoon soy sauce
1 slice ginger
¼ cup water or chicken stock
Pinch of sugar
½ cup sliced bamboo shoots *or* 2 inches peeled cucumber
1 tablespoon mayonnaise
½ teaspoon Asian sesame oil
½ teaspoon mild vinegar
1 cup shredded cooked chicken

Soak the mushrooms in lukewarm water until they are soft and swollen, about 20 minutes. Drain, cut off and discard the stems, and cut the caps into thin strips. Place the strips in a small saucepan with the soy sauce, ginger, stock, and sugar. Simmer until the liquid is reduced to less than a tablespoon. Drain, reserving the liquid, and let cool.

Meanwhile, cut the bamboo shoots or cucumber into matchstick-size pieces. Combine the mayonnaise, sesame oil, and vinegar and stir in a teaspoon or so of the reserved mushroom soy sauce. Add the mushrooms, bamboo shoots, and chicken and toss to coat. Adjust the seasoning and spread thickly on room-temperature bagel halves.

Makes 1½ cups, enough for 2 bagels

Best on sesame bagels.

SASHIMI BAGEL

This is certainly the most offbeat recipe in the book, but sashimi (Japanese-style raw fish) actually tastes and looks great on a bagel. Tuna and either farm-raised or frozen salmon are probably your best fish choices. If there is a Japanese fish market nearby, ask them what other fish they have are suitable for sashimi. (You don't have to tell them you're planning to put it on bagels.) Whatever the fish, it should be sparkling fresh with no trace of fishy smell. An Asian market or fish store is the best place to find the wasabi (powdered green horseradish) and pinkish pickled ginger.

---

1 teaspoon wasabi powder
2 tablespoons cream cheese, softened
Soy sauce
1 sesame bagel, cut into 4 slices
3 ounces sashimi-grade raw fish
Japanese pickled ginger, for garnish

Measure the wasabi powder into a large spoon and mix in a few drops of water, just enough to make a paste. Work the wasabi paste into the cream cheese, then add soy sauce (just a little) to taste. Spread the cheese on the bagel slices. Cut the fish into triangular or rectangular pieces no more than an inch thick, then slice them thinly across the grain. Arrange the slices on top of the cheese in a flower-petal pattern. Add a few slices of pickled ginger and serve open-face.

Serves 2

"CHEESE DANISH"

What makes Danish pastry taste the way it does (besides lots of butter) is cardamom, an Indian spice. It tastes much better if freshly ground, but you don't need a mortar and pestle or special spice grinder. Just put the seeds in a small bowl or coffee cup and crush them with the back of a spoon. Try these bagel pastries with morning coffee or afternoon tea.

½ cup farmer's cheese, drained cottage cheese, or ricotta
2 teaspoons sugar
Seeds from 1 cardamom pod, ground
1 egg yolk
2 very fresh bagels
4 dried prunes or apricots or pecan halves

Preheat the oven to 350°F. Combine the cheese, sugar, cardamom, and egg yolk and beat until smooth. Split the bagels and plug the holes with dried fruit or pecans. Spread a quarter of the cheese mixture on each bagel half, spreading all the way to the edges. Bake on an ungreased cookie sheet until the cheese is set and beginning to crack, 13 to 15 minutes. Serve warm.

Extremely Easy Variation:
Spread slightly warm bagel halves with cream cheese and sprinkle with freshly ground cardamom.

Makes 4 pastries

Best with cinnamon raisin, blueberry, or other fruit-studded bagels.

HONEY-CHEESE BRUSCHETTA

I first tasted *bruschetta* with honey and cheese in 1983 at Badia a Coltibuono in Tuscany. They made it with their famous olive oil, honey from their own chestnut trees, and Pecorino Toscanello, a firm but sliceable sheep's milk cheese which has been imported here from time to time. If you can find Pecorino Toscanello, great. If not, use a domestic aged asiago, Gruyère, or a mixture of either with a little Pecorino Romano.

---

2 ounces cheese (see above)
2 plain or sesame bagels, split
1 to 2 tablespoons extra virgin olive oil
1 to 2 tablespoons dark, flavorful honey

With a cheese plane or vegetable peeler, cut off enough thin strips of the cheese to cover the bagel halves, but don't put it on yet. Broil the bagel halves until lightly toasted and brush them with a little oil. Top each with cheese and return them to the broiler until the cheese melts slightly. Drizzle on the honey and eat the bagels warm, with a glass of good red wine.

Serves 2 to 4

BLUEBERRY AND MANGO BAGEL

I resisted the idea of blueberry bagels as long as I could, but now I guess they are no weirder than blueberry muffins. One of my favorite fruit combinations is mango and blueberry. I tried it with a blueberry bagel and, you know, it's good.

---

1 ripe medium-size mango
½ teaspoon minced or grated ginger
1 tablespoon lime or lemon juice
2 blueberry bagels, split

Cut the mango flesh away from the pit and into strips an inch or so wide; place them skin side down on a cutting board and cut the flesh away from the skin. Cut the strips into ¼-inch cubes and combine them with the ginger and lime juice. Spread the mango mixture, including any juices that collect in the bowl, on the bagel halves, mashing it a little as you spread it.

Serves 2

RAISIN BAGEL PUDDING

Cinnamon raisin is one of the most popular bagel "flavors." The first time I bought them I found they were too sweet for me for breakfast. So I decided to try making them into dessert. Here's the result — a delicious bread pudding.

———

4 cinnamon raisin bagels
5 eggs
⅓ cup sugar
2½ cups whole milk or half-and-half
½ teaspoon vanilla extract
¼ teaspoon nutmeg
⅛ teaspoon ground cloves
1 large apple, peeled and sliced (optional)

Cut the unsliced bagels in half (semicircles), then cut each half crosswise into slices about ⅓ inch thick. Because of the curve of the bagel, the slices will be all different shapes; that's okay. Cut any especially large ones in half. Set aside.

Beat the eggs and sugar together in a large mixing bowl. Beat in the milk, vanilla, nutmeg, and cloves. Add the bagel slices, toss to moisten them evenly, and set aside to soak for 15 minutes.

Preheat the oven to 375°F. Set a roasting pan in the oven and have hot water ready. Spoon the pudding mixture into an 8-cup soufflé dish. Place it in the roasting pan and add hot water to come about halfway up the sides of the dish. Bake until a knife inserted in the center comes out clean, 35 to 40 minutes. Let cool a while; serve warm.

Serves 8 to 10

———

Bagels are now being sold in supermarkets across the country, but there may still be places where this delectable bread is unavailable. For those living outside bagel territory, and for all you dedicated do-it-yourselfers, here is a recipe for darned good homemade bagels.

1½ cups warm (100°F) water
1 tablespoon active dry yeast
4 teaspoons kosher salt
2 tablespoons mild vegetable oil
4½ cups (approximately) all-purpose flour
1 egg, beaten with a pinch of salt and sugar
¼ cup sesame or poppy seeds (optional)

Mixing: Warm a medium mixing bowl and add the warm water. Sprinkle in the yeast and let stand until the yeast sinks. Stir in the salt and oil, then 4 cups of the flour. Stir until the mixture becomes too heavy and sticky, then turn it out onto a lightly floured board. Knead, adding more flour as necessary to keep the dough from sticking, until it is smooth and elastic, about 10 minutes. Cover the dough loosely with a clean, dry towel and let it rest 10 minutes.

Shaping: Divide the dough in half, then divide each half into four pieces. Roll each piece of dough gently into a ball. Lay a ball of dough on a lightly floured surface, dip a fingertip in flour, and press down into the center to make a hole. Twirl the bagel around your finger, either up in the air or down against the board, to expand the hole to at least 1½ inches and stretch out the circle to about 3½ inches. Place the bagels 2 inches apart on cookie sheets lined with baking parchment. Cover with towels and set in a warm, draft-free place until the bagels have risen noticeably, 30 to 45 minutes.

Boiling: Preheat the oven to 375°F. Bring a large pot of water to a boil. Carefully lift a bagel off the paper, drop it into the boiling water, and boil 30 seconds. Remove it with a skimmer or slotted spatula and put it back on the cookie sheet. Repeat with the remaining bagels.

Baking: Brush the egg mixture lightly all over the tops and sides of the bagels. Sprinkle with poppy or sesame seeds, if you like. Bake until golden brown, 18 to 20 minutes, turning the pan midway through baking so they brown evenly. Let cool on a wire rack before slicing, if you can stand to wait that long.

Makes 8 large (4-ounce) bagels

For 12 medium (3-ounce) bagels, divide the dough into 12 pieces instead of 8.

BAGEL CHIPS

These are nothing more than bagels sliced very thin and toasted cracker-crisp, so they can be used for dipping. I am sure they were invented by some thrifty bagel baker or deli owner as a way to turn leftover bagels into something salable. Slicing the bagels is easiest with an electric slicer, which I know is not found in every home kitchen. A food processor is another possibility, if you don't care about maintaining the round shape. There will be a lot of waste this way, in pieces too thin to use. If you're really good with a knife, you can cut them by hand.

Day-old bagels

Cut each bagel into about ten ⅛-inch-thick slices. (To do this with a food processor, cut the bagels to the largest size that will fit in your feed tube and use a 4mm slicing blade.) Preheat the oven to 300°F. Lay the slices in a single layer on cookie sheets and bake them until lightly browned in the center and medium brown around the thinnest edges, about 10 minutes. If your slices are not quite even in thickness, start checking after 5 to 7 minutes and pull off the ones that are browning ahead of the others. Let your chips cool on the pans, then store them in a paper or plastic bag.

1 bagel yields about 10 large chips

Best with plain bagels, but any non-sweet variety will work.

BAGEL CROUTONS

Croutons are a time-honored way of using up stale bread. They're great in salads. I also like them for scooping up dips and just plain munching. If you use seeded bagels, brush off as many seeds as possible so they won't fall off and burn in the baking pan.

**1 bagel
2 tablespoons olive oil
Large pinch of salt**

Preheat the oven to 300°F. Cut the unsliced bagel in half (semicircles), then cut each half crosswise into slices a bit less than ¼ inch thick. Because of the curving shape, the slices will be different shapes; that's okay, as long as they are the same thickness. Discard the end pieces that are mostly crust. Lay the slices on a cookie sheet. Drizzle with the oil. Turn the pieces over and move them around to oil them as evenly as possible. Sprinkle with salt and bake until golden brown and crisp, 10 to 12 minutes. Drain on paper towels.

Garlic Croutons:
Bruise a clove of garlic and set it in the oil to steep for half an hour. Remove it before oiling the bagel slices.

Makes about 2 dozen croutons

Good with any non-sweet bagel.

BAGEL STUFFING
FOR POULTRY

This recipe is based on a stuffing described to me by Noah Alper, founder of Berkeley-based Noah's Bagels. It's best to use a variety of bagels and good crusty bread; a stuffing made from bagels alone will be too heavy. Include at least one rye or pumpernickel bagel or several slices of rye bread for a good depth of flavor. Onion or garlic bagels are also good. Of course, you should add whatever tidbits have always made your stuffing special and distinctive.

---

1 or 2 stale bagels
2 slices stale bread
1 tablespoon oil
½ cup diced onion
½ cup finely diced celery
2 cloves garlic, finely chopped
¼ cup chopped parsley
¼ teaspoon dried thyme or mixed *herbes de Provence*
½ cup chicken stock (canned or homemade)
Salt and freshly ground pepper to taste

Cut the bagels and bread into small cubes (¼ to ⅜ inch or less). Cut enough to make 2 cups. If they're not good and stale already, spread the cubes out on a cookie sheet for a couple of hours to overnight. Combine the oil, onion, celery, and garlic in a large skillet over medium heat. Cook until the onion is soft but not browned. Stir in the herbs and stock, then the bread and bagel cubes. Toss to moisten the cubes evenly, taste for seasoning, and correct if necessary. Let cool before stuffing the bird.

Makes 2 cups, enough for a large roasting chicken
Double or triple the recipe for a turkey.

WHAT A BAGEL CAN'T DO

As adaptable as they are, there are a few things a bagel shouldn't be asked to do. Here is a short list of bagel don'ts:

The Bagel Burger: A hamburger bun needs to be large enough to enclose the meat patty and all its garnishes, and soft and compressible enough to collapse slightly when you bite into it. It should also be very absorbent, to drink up the juices from the meat. If you think these qualities don't sound like a bagel, you're right.

The Dagwood Bagel: Despite the yearnings our cover illustration may stir, you can't pile all sorts of things on a bagel half and cover it with the other half to make a sandwich. Not successfully anyway. Leaving aside the question of jumbled flavors, the incompressible texture of a good bagel makes it inappropriate for any but the thinnest of sandwich fillings.

Bagel French Toast: Suffice it to say that if your bagels are soft and absorbent enough to soak up the egg and cook to a fork-tender consistency, they're not very good bagels.

BAGEL MENUS

A bowl or basket of sliced bagels can be the centerpiece of a memorable breakfast, brunch, or lunch. Whether you're having a friend or two drop by on a weekend or you're throwing a party for twenty, it's easy to build your menu around bagels and things to spread on them. Three such menus follow — a traditional Sunday brunch of bagels and lox, a buffet that is anything but traditional (and definitely not kosher), and a Thanksgiving weekend brunch with bagels and leftover turkey sharing top billing.

If your friends like bagels as much as mine do, figure on two bagels per person. You may have some left over, but that's better than running out. If at all possible, arrange to buy the bagels fresh that morning. Day-old bagels can be refreshed by warming them slightly in a low oven, but once they cool off they will be as stale as before. Don't slice all the bagels right away. It's better to put out an assortment at first and replenish the basket as necessary.

If you're putting out a variety of spreads and toppings on a buffet, lay out more forks and knives than you think you need. Someone is bound to walk off with the lox serving fork on his plate, and the most popular spread will end up with four spreading knives in it.

Not every recipe in this book is suitable for buffet serving. Avoid those that take a lot of assembly, like the Muffuletta Bagel, or those with loose toppings that might fall off, like the Chicken Shiitake Salad.

Don't feel you have to offer all of the dishes listed in a menu; use as many as you like, with an eye to variety of flavors. Add your choice of fruit, juices, coffee or other drinks, and anything else you think will add pleasure.

You can, of course, make this menu part of an even more elaborate brunch spread, with eggs or other hot dishes. Personally, I'm happy to let the bagels and lox be the main event.

Bagels (assorted flavors)

Cream cheese or Fromage Blanc (page 12)

Smoked salmon, 1 to 2 ounces per person, thinly sliced
Your choice of:
Cold-smoked salmon (page 114)
Belly lox
Home-Cured Salmon (page 30)
or Gravlax (page 31)

Sliced tomatoes

Thinly sliced onions, raw or pickled (page 59)

Thinly sliced cucumbers

Capers

Lemon wedges

BAGEL BUFFET

Here is a menu of decidedly non-traditional bagel toppings. This buffet is more appropriate for lunch than breakfast. For that matter, it would be perfect for any casual afternoon or evening party.

Assorted bagels

Cream cheese or Fromage Blanc (page 12)

Orange marmalade

Prune or Apricot-Almond Cream Cheese (page 15,17)

Shrimp or Lobster Salad (page 35)

Deviled Ham (page 39)

"Refried" Beans (page 69) with grated cheese

Satay-Style Chicken (page 80) with Spicy Peanut Sauce (page 81)

The long weekend after Thanksgiving is a great time for brunches. Here's a menu featuring bagels and leftover turkey. If you feel cream cheese is too rich after the big feed, leave it out. As long as your bagels are good and fresh, a thick spread of cranberry sauce, chutney or hummus, or an eggplant spread is really all you need to moisten a turkey-topped bagel.

Assorted bagels

Cream cheese or Yogurt Cheese (page 13)

Thinly sliced roast turkey

Cranberry sauce

Chutney or Onion Marmalade (page 58)

Hummus (page 75)

A roasted eggplant spread (see pages 50-53)

Peeled and sliced navel oranges

WHAT IS A BAGEL?

Basically a bagel is a doughnut-shaped roll that's dense inside and has a chewy crust outside. Bagels originated in central Europe (according to most accounts, in Vienna) around the end of the 17th century. The name is Yiddish, and comes from a Middle High German word for ring or bracelet. Those are the technical facts. But what makes a bagel a bagel, and not just another hunk of bread? The fact that it is boiled before it goes into the oven. Boiling creates a skin on the dough which limits how much it can expand during baking. So you get the dense texture and chewy crust we all love.

Today some commercial bakers steam their bagels instead of boiling them. They say it gives their bagels a longer shelf life, and it's certainly more efficient for large-scale production. Traditionalists insist that steamed bagels have inferior texture, and they lament that the proliferation of steaming means nobody knows what a bagel should taste like anymore. The fact is, there are excellent bagels and mediocre bagels made by both methods. So find a brand you like and don't worry about how they're cooked.

ANY WAY YOU SLICE IT

If you think of a bagel as a doughnut with backbone, I suppose it makes perfect sense to eat it like a doughnut, either chomping down on the whole thing or breaking off pieces that are easier to eat from one end (also easier to dunk in coffee). I have been known to eat bagels this way, especially the sweeter varieties. But most of the time the first step in eating a bagel is to slice it in half, revealing those two flat inner surfaces that beg for a topping. Slicing a bagel is no more difficult or dangerous than any other kitchen chore that involves a knife — and no less so.

First, the knife. If you have a serrated bread knife, it will work fine. And if your bagels are fresh, a really sharp non-serrated chef's knife will do the job quite well. Either way, a long blade makes the job easier; it allows you to cut with one or two strokes of the knife rather than endless sawing back and forth. (My wife always gasps when I pull out a knife with a 10-inch blade for a small cutting task, but it really is easier to use than a smaller one.)

There are two schools of thought on bagel slicing technique: the horizontal and the vertical. I'm a vertical type myself. If there is a scar on the edge of the bagel where it touched the one next to it on the baking pan, set that part down against the cutting board for more stability. Hold the bagel near the top from above, between thumb and fingers, and carefully start the cut with the edge (not the point) of the knife. This is where the sharpness of the blade is critical; if it's dull it may slip and cut your fingers or thumb, but if it's good and sharp it will start right into the bagel. As you cut down through the bagel, make sure your fingers don't slip into the hole in the middle.

Some people prefer to lay the bagel on the board and hold the knife horizontally, slicing parallel to the board. This works, but I find it slower. [Excuse me. This is his wife, one of those "some people" he's talking about. I cut horizontally. It feels safer. And I always use a serrated knife. It's not slower at all.] Again, the key is to hold the bagel still while keeping your fingers out of harm's way. The best way is to hold the bagel with the palm of your hand, fingers arched back out of the way.

You may find a combination of the two techniques the best way to go — start with a horizontal cut, then when the knife is well started, turn the bagel up on its rim and finish with a vertical cut.

In recent years a kitchen gadget called a bagel slicer has hit the market. It is a holder made of wood or plastic that keeps the bagel from slipping while you cut it. Some versions even have different settings, for thicker and thinner bagels or multiple slices. I don't have one, but I have friends who swear by them.

If you're out of the house and you're hungry and all you have is a pocket knife, plunge the point in from the rim to the center, then hold and rotate the bagel as you saw your way around in a circle. This tends to produce a raggedy cut, but who cares?

HOLLOWING (THE TUNNEL BAGEL)

The bagel was not designed to be a sandwich roll. By the time you slice it in half, heap it with filling, and put the top half back on top, the whole thing is likely to be too thick to fit in your mouth. Bagels aren't as compressible as other breads, so as you squeeze one side to take a bite, any slippery filling is going to come splooshing out the other side.

I almost always recommend putting a topping on two bagel halves rather than filling the bagel like a sandwich. But I know some of you are going to insist on turning your bagel into a stuffed sandwich no matter what I say, so let me pass on a tip from Mexican sandwich shops: hollow the bagel out first to make more room.

For one bagel, you'll need about ⅓ cup of a soft sandwich filling. You can use tuna salad, salmon salad, chicken salad, chopped herring, eggplant spread, hummus, or any other easily spreadable filling. Slice the bagel in half. Pinch off and pull away some of the bready interior from each half, leaving a shallow groove. Line the grooves with soft lettuce leaves if you like. Then spread the filling in one of the grooves, heaping it slightly. Top with the other bagel half, enclosing all the filling in your secret tunnel.

TOASTING TECHNIQUES

If you are lucky enough to live near a bagel bakery, and your timing is right, you can have the incomparable experience of bagels still warm from the oven. Otherwise, you can eat your bagels at room temperature, or you can explore with me the various possible ways to warm them to a much more satisfying temperature.

The toaster is an obvious answer to the warming question, but it does have problems. My toaster can handle only one bagel at a time. Not very convenient for a crowd, or even a family of three. Some older toasters are so narrow they won't take even one of the hefty bagels I'm partial to, unless you slice them disturbingly thin. I've noticed that newer toasters and supermarket bagels each seem to have been designed with the other in mind — the toaster openings are somewhat wider, the bagels somewhat thinner. So if you have that kind of toaster and that kind of bagel, and one at a time is enough, your problem is solved.

Toaster ovens and broilers are good alternatives to the toaster, though you have to turn the bagels if you want to toast both sides. If you are going to use the broiler for, say, a cheese-topped bagel, you might as well do the preliminary toasting under the broiler too.

Personally, I like to warm whole bagels in a low oven, which restores some of their original texture without the crispness of toasting. The oven is also ideal for frozen bagels; pop them in right from the freezer and they come out fresh-tasting and warm.

How much to toast is a matter of taste. Sometimes I like the added crunch of a crisp toasted surface, sometimes I don't. The texture of the other ingredients may dictate; a crunchy bagel offers a nice contrast to a soft tuna salad, for example.

Then there's the question of serving temperature, especially when cream cheese is involved. Spread cream cheese on a bagel hot from the toaster and watch the transformation. You'll have to decide for yourself if it's a good thing or not. (There's strong disagreement in our family on this.)

A note of caution: For some reason, the smooth surface of a plain bagel comes out of the toaster or oven hotter than any other kind of toast, hot enough to burn your fingers. The poppy or sesame seeds on a seeded bagel create an insulating layer, but watch out for those smooth ones!

If you take bagels along on a camping trip (a delicious idea), you can toast them over the campfire, either on a grate or on a stick, marshmallow style. Remember, I said over the fire, not in it.

HOLE PLUGGERS

Sometimes the hole in the middle of the bagel can be big enough for your topping to fall through, or at least ooze through so it ends up on your fingers. Here are some ideas for edible things that can hold the space while you spread on the rest of the topping, and that taste good, too. Some are small enough to hide under the topping as a surprise while others stand up like the flag on a golf green. Choose one that is compatible with the topping you're serving — pickled pepper doesn't make much sense with cream cheese and jelly.

- **AN OLIVE** — Black or green, pitted or whole

- **A RADISH** — Leaves trimmed to a short handle

- **A CUCUMBER CONE** — Cut a thin slice from a good-sized cuke; make a cut from the edge to the center, then overlap the cut parts to form a cone.

- **A SCALLION FLOWER** — Cut a 1-inch section from the white or pale green part of a scallion. Make numerous cuts from the middle out to one end with the tip of a paring knife or by inserting a needle and dragging it toward the end. Place the piece in a bowl of cold water until the cut parts curl back, like petals. Fancy-shmancy.

- **A CAULIFLOWER OR BROCCOLI FLORET** — With a longish stem, blanched or raw

- **A PICKLED PEPPER** — Cherry, jalapeño, peperoncini

- **A GRAPE OR CHERRY** — For bagels with sweet topping

- **A MINIATURE TOMATO** — Cherry or pear shape

- **A *CORNICHON* OR GHERKIN** — For a bagel with a small hole

- **A CARROT FLOWER** — Peel a good-sized carrot and trim the end to a blunt point. About an inch above the point, work your way around the carrot making 4 or 5 overlapping cuts, at the same angle as the point cuts, almost meeting at the point. Twist the "flower" to pull it loose. (This will take some practice, but once you get it it's a handy garnish for lots of things.)

- **A DILL PICKLE FLOWER** — Made like the carrot flower above

STORING WITHOUT STALING

If your bagels come in a plastic bag, that's the best way to store them. I mostly buy mine from a bagel bakery which gives them to me in a paper bag. I put the paper bag inside a plastic bag, and the bagels stay fresh for a day or two. Even on the third day they can be revived by toasting or warming in the oven. To keep bagels any longer than that, it's best to freeze them in a plastic bag. (Refrigerator temperatures actually make breads go stale faster than either keeping them at room temperature or freezing and thawing them.)

If you are planning to toast your bagels after freezing, slice them before you store them. It is barely possible to slice a frozen bagel, but it's about a hundred times more difficult and dangerous than slicing a fresh one. I prefer to leave the bagels whole and thaw them in the oven. Lay them on a cookie sheet, place it in a cold oven, turn the heat on to 300°, and bake about 10 minutes. Remove the bagels from the oven and give them a few minutes for the heat to reach all the way to the center.

THE BROWN-BAG BAGEL

Lots of the recipes in this book are suitable lunches for work or school. (More often than not a bagel from Sunday's dozen is in my daughter's lunch box on Monday.)

Packing your own bagel lunch will not only save you money, it will give you more control over what you eat. Most delis slather on too much cream cheese for my taste — they figure they have to give you your money's worth. You can ask them to put on less, but they'll still charge you the same amount. If you make your own "shmeer," you can use just as much as you like.

Cream cheese-filled bagels can be assembled hours ahead of time, but some other toppings might be too wet to leave in contact with the bagel all morning. The Shrimp or Lobster Salad on page 35, for example, is pretty wet, so it's better to take it in a separate container and put in on your bagel just before eating.

In the best of all possible worlds we would all have a deli or bakery close by, so we could pick up a freshly baked bagel in the morning or at lunch hour. If you're one of the lucky ones who does, have them slice it in half, then when you're ready to eat just add your favorite topping or sandwich filling.

If your office lunch room or coffee station has a microwave oven, you can use it to reheat some of the hot recipes in this book. Even if you are going to eat it sandwich style, leave the top half of the bagel off so you reheat mostly the filling. The heat the sandwich gives off will warm the top when you put it back together. Depending on the power of your oven, 30 to 40 seconds at full power should do for reheating most things. The following recipes are perfect for heating in a microwave oven:

- Reuben Bagel (page 42) — Assemble at home, but don't heat until lunchtime.

- Hot Pastrami (page 43) — It's best to heat the pastrami for a full minute separately to cook off some of the fat. Drain the meat on a paper towel, then put it on the bagel and heat the whole thing a little more.

- Wurst and Eggs (page 41) — Assemble at home; heat at lunchtime.

- Scrambled Egg and Cheese (page 25) — Ditto.

- "Refried" Beans (page 69) — Carry the grated cheese separately; heat open-face.

- Bagel Pizza (page 76) or Green Chile and Jack (page 78) — Take the ingredients along separately and assemble just before cooking. The cheese will melt but not brown.

INGREDIENT TIPS

- CHICK-PEAS — Canned chick-peas (garbanzo beans) are convenient and usually very good. If you're a purist, you can buy dry chick-peas, soak them overnight, and cook them yourself. Use ¾ cup dried peas to yield 2 cups cooked.

- CREAM CHEESE — If you are one of those fortunate people for whom fat doesn't matter, by all means use real cream cheese. If fat does matter, consider the lower-fat alternatives. "Light" cream cheese (domestic Neufchâtel) is made with a higher proportion of milk to cream. It's what I use at home, and I really don't miss the fat. For an even lower-fat alternative, you can make *fromage blanc*, a blend of ricotta and plain yogurt. (See recipe, page 12). For a zero-fat option, try making the yogurt cheese on page 13 with nonfat yogurt. Most cream cheese these days is very smooth because it contains gum arabic or other vegetable gums which are added to improve the texture. In some delis and specialty cheese shops you'll find cream cheese in large cylindrical tubes, to be cut and weighed in chunks like liverwurst. This type doesn't have vegetable gums, so the texture may look a little crumbly, but it spreads beautifully.

- FETA — A tangy and salty white cheese, usually made from sheep's milk. It is stored and shipped in brine. The best versions come from Greece, Bulgaria, and Corsica. If possible, keep it in some of its original brine in the refrigerator.

- GARAM MASALA — An Indian blend of sweet and "warm" spices. You can buy it ready-made in Indian markets and some spice shops, or make your own. Formulas vary. Mine is 2 parts *each* ground black pepper, cardamom, coriander, and cumin to 1 part *each* cinnamon and ground cloves.

- JICAMA (pronounced HEE-ka-ma) — Look for this tuber, shaped like an oversized turnip but with dull brownish skin, where Mexican or Chinese foods are sold. Peel off the skin to reveal translucent white flesh with an apple-like texture and a taste somewhere between sweet and bland. Store any unused portion in the refrigerator and use it as soon as possible. (Try it in place of water chestnuts in a stir-fry.)

- LOX (cold-smoked salmon) — The most famous bagel topping of all, after cream cheese, is smoked salmon. Not just any smoked salmon, but the moist, tender, thin-sliceable cold-smoked variety usually known as lox, after the Russian word for salmon.

  Not all smoked salmon is lox; in fact, some would argue that no smoked salmon is lox. One long-time Brooklyn salmon processor uses the name lox to refer to salt-cured *unsmoked* salmon. They call their smoked version "Nova" (short for Nova Scotia, where a lot of the smoked salmon sold in New York once came from). However, this distinction is almost unknown these days, and may be dying out.

  Whatever you call it, the kind of fish I am talking about is cured with salt and usually some sugar to draw out the excess moisture. It is then partially dried in a smokehouse at a relatively low temperature (under 100°). What makes each brand of smoked salmon unique is the kind of salmon used (Atlantic or Pacific), the amount of salt and sugar, other curing ingredients such as spices and liquors, and the time and temperature of curing and smoking. Shop around to find your favorite.

  High-quality lox is expensive, twenty to thirty dollars a pound where I live, but there are some cheaper alternatives. "Belly lox" is made from the strip of fatter belly meat on a salmon filet; it's usually saltier and less delicate in taste, but a good deal cheaper. Some delis also sell odds and ends of more expensive cuts as "lox trim" for a lower price. Hot-smoked fish (see page 29) is another possibility entirely.

  The irony is that cheaper grades of lox, being saltier, go a lot farther; a few small patches can be enough to top half a bagel.With the more expensive, more delicate type, you can cover the whole surface of the bagel and still have a milder flavor — and spend four or five times as much money.

Traditional accompaniments to lox and bagels, besides a layer of cream cheese, include thinly sliced raw onion and sliced tomato. Cucumbers, capers, or a squeeze of lemon juice are also possibilities.

- PEPPERS, ROASTING AND PEELING — To remove the waxy, rather indigestible outer skin from bell peppers or large chiles, rub them lightly with oil and bake them on a cookie sheet in a 350° or hotter oven until the skins are blistered all over. Or put the peppers under the broiler or on the barbecue to cook, turning them as the skins blister and darken. When blackened, transfer the peppers to a bowl and cover them so they steam for a while as they cool. The skins should slip off easily. Slit the peeled peppers open and remove the seeds and ribs.

  Sweet red peppers are available already roasted and peeled in jars, but the citric acid used in the processing can overwhelm their natural sweetness. I use them only as a last resort.

- SUN-DRIED TOMATOES — Once available only in expensive jars from Italy, dried tomatoes are now produced in this country. The Italian oil-packed variety still sets the flavor standard, but the domestic versions get better and more widely available every year. The cheapest way to go is to buy the tomatoes dry and reconstitute them yourself as needed.

- TAHINI — A ground sesame paste used throughout the Middle East. It's easiest to find in health food stores. I use the toasted version, but raw tahini is also fine.

INDEX

Metric Conversion Table

Follow this chart to convert the measurements in this book to their approximate metric equivalents. The metric amounts have been rounded; the slight variations in the conversion rate will not significantly change the recipes.

Liquid and Dry Volume	Metric Equivalent	Temperature	
		°Fahrenheit	°Celsius
1 teaspoon	5 ml	155	70
1 tablespoon (3 teaspoons)	15 ml	165	75
¼ cup	60 ml	185	85
⅓ cup	80 ml	200	95
½ cup	125 ml	275	135
1 cup	250 ml	300	150
		325	160
Weight		350	175
1 ounce	28 grams	375	190
¼ pound	113 grams	400	205
½ pound	225 grams	450	230
1 pound	450 grams		

Linear

1 inch	2.5 cm

Other Helpful Conversion Factors

Sugar, Rice, Flour	1 teaspoon = 10 grams
	1 cup = 220 grams
Cornstarch, Salt	1 teaspoon = 5 grams
	1 tablespoon = 15 grams